Advance Praise for *The Eclipse Effect*

"*The Eclipse Effect* reminds us that real leadership isn't about titles or top-down authority—it's about rolling up your sleeves and building something that matters, together. Through the lens of the extraordinary communities that sprang up around recent total solar eclipses, this book explores how shared moments can grow into lasting movements. It's a powerful guide for anyone—whether you're just starting out or already leading—who wants to make a difference through hard work, openness, and trust. Most of all, it challenges us to imagine a better future—and offers a clear, grounded path for making it real."

— Jimmy Wales, founder of Wikipedia
and author of *The Seven Rules of Trust*

I0112668

THE
ECLIPSE
EFFECT

THE
ECLIPSE
EFFECT

How to Seize Extraordinary Moments to Build Strong Communities

Jamie Carter & Debra Ross

POST Hill
PRESS

A POST HILL PRESS BOOK
ISBN: 979-8-89565-107-0
ISBN (eBook): 979-8-89565-108-7

The Eclipse Effect:
How to Seize Extraordinary Moments to Build Strong Communities
© 2025 by Jamie Carter & Debra Ross
All Rights Reserved

Cover design by Tyler Nordgren

Post Hill Press
New York • Nashville
posthillpress.com

Published in the United States of America
1 2 3 4 5 6 7 8 9 10

To my daughter Ella, who started me on this journey; to my daughter Madison, who helped me across the finish line; and to my husband David, who, despite what it may have looked like, never actually thought I was crazy.
— Debra Ross

To my wife Gill, who eclipses me every day.
— Jamie Carter

Table of Contents

Introduction

In the fall of 2012, my daughter Ella attended a middle school astronomy class at the Strasenburgh Planetarium of the Rochester Museum & Science Center (RMSC). One day after class, she hopped in the car and announced, "In five years, I'll be sixteen. I'll have my driver's license, and you and I will take a road trip to Missouri."

"Sure," I answered, privately thinking, *Who plans for anything five years in the future?* (And, *Missouri?*)

Ella's class had just learned that on August 21, 2017, a total solar eclipse—the first major one in the continental United States since 1979—would start in Oregon and, over the course of an hour and a half, travel diagonally across the country and exit at the South Carolina shore. A total solar eclipse occurs when the Moon passes directly between the Earth and the Sun, briefly blocking sunlight. While *partial* solar eclipses happen globally about twice a year and can be seen across a wide area of the globe, *total* solar eclipses are less frequent and can only be fully experienced within a very narrow path of totality.

"It's going to pass just south of St. Louis," Ella reported. "You like St. Louis. So that's where we'll go."

"Sure," I answered again, smiling to myself.

"But seven years later, on April 8, 2024," she continued, "there will be another total solar eclipse in the US. For that one, the path of totality will pass right over Rochester. I'll be an adult by then, but I'll come back home for it."

For the following five years, I remained an eclipse skeptic. *People seem to go nuts for this*, I thought. *It gets dark every night. I know what a shadow is. What's the big deal?* As August 2017 drew nearer and Ella planned the trip, I was enthusiastic, but mostly at the prospect of spending a few days together nurturing her passion for science.

What I didn't expect was that the moments Ella and I would spend in totality on that steamy August day in Kimmswick, Missouri, would, for me, become one of those bifurcation points in life where a sudden force changes your momentum and launches you in an entirely new direction. As Ella and I watched the Moon gradually cover the Sun's bright disc through our eclipse glasses, I grew to appreciate what the fuss was about. All of the astronomy and solar system textbook knowledge I'd amassed since third grade suddenly became something I was experiencing in my whole body rather than just in my brain. In the last minute before totality, the light around us grew silvery and glittery, the birds flew back to their nests, and the crickets started chirping. The moment the Moon completely covered the Sun, the world around us blurred and dimmed. Then it was safe to remove the glasses and look up. As I gazed at what seemed to be a velvet hole in the sky, I was tinglingly aware of only four bodies in the entire universe: the Sun, the Moon, the Earth, and me. *I* was one of those bodies. While some report feeling humbled when faced with the vastness of space, I experienced a profound sense of the significance of humans' place in the universe and our ability to understand it.

A minute and a half later, the Sun emerged from behind the Moon, and, as Ella likes to say, "My mother went a little crazy." In just seven short years, our hometown would be in totality for three minutes and thirty-eight seconds. Someone needed to start preparing the Rochester community to make the most of the gift the universe was granting us, and it might as well be me. The Rochester Eclipse Task Force formed in my head on the drive home from Missouri, and I first started tagging people to be part of it the following month.

Why me?

In part, it was because my particular profession gave me unique access to resources that were to be invaluable in the seven-year effort. In 2001, shortly after Ella was born, I had founded KidsOutAndAbout.com, a website that helps families across North America discover and connect with local events, activities, and community opportunities. The network began expanding beyond Rochester in 2010, and it now serves parents coast-to-coast in the United States and Canada. As publisher and CEO, I lead a team that runs the business, but I remain a passionate cheerleader for all things Rochester. I had many dozens of connections within our area from which to recruit participants and other leaders. I had developed a self-driven work ethic that didn't rely on external validation; plus, the autonomy of being a business owner allowed me to dedicate myself fully to what became a second full-time job. Celebrating this community for the past quarter-century has blessed me with countless personal connections with the people who make things happen here, and they know that if they do great things, I'll shout about them to people who will listen.

Publishing KidsOutAndAbout.com has given me a unique window through which to view a wide range of communities across North America—large and small, for-profit and non-profit, thriving and struggling. Having this vantage point has allowed me to think deeply about what makes some communities flourish while others falter, insights that have shaped many of the strategies shared in this book. I first applied these strategies within my own business team, then in community leadership roles, and ultimately with the eclipse task force.

But more than anything, I was fueled by a passion sparked by the eclipse: a desire to help others experience the awe and wonder I had felt. I felt certain that our region could succeed in 2024 as other path communities had in 2017, and was ready to put in the work to make it happen. My role was to connect people, build dashboards and newsletters, and bring what my children call my "painfully cheerful" energy to meetings. My ultimate goal was to celebrate the individuals who drive our community forward, encouraging them to seize this opportunity not just for their own businesses and organizations, but to help the Rochester area shine in its moment in the shadow and secure its place in history as a connected community who made the most of this once-in-a-century opportunity.

Of course, leading the task force was never something I intended to do alone. As our region's main informal science learning hub, the RMSC knew, decades ahead of everyone else, that the eclipse presented an opportunity both for our community and for science learning and connection. They were the main backbone of the effort here in Rochester: They not only implemented systems of education and outreach for their own programs, but they also sponsored the task force with rooms for our in-person meetings, provided technology both for meetings and for outreach, made connections to educators, industry, and funders, and, most important, had people with brains and passion.

Equally useful in community organizing for the eclipse was my upcoming role as chair of Visit Rochester's Visitor Industry Council (VIC), the member-driven arm of our region's destination marketing organization. The leadership of Visit Rochester had seen the data from communities in the 2017 path and immediately grasped its potential for our area, both for visitor influx and for visibility on the national stage. The way Visit Rochester had structured and nurtured the VIC since the early 1980s made it the perfect model for the eclipse task force. I've been an enthusiastic member of the VIC since about 2010; as its 2018 chair, I started each of our monthly VIC meetings with, "What's happening in Rochester on April 8, 2024?" Although it was still six years in our future, everyone knew the answer by the March meeting.

The Rochester area also had a resource that other communities lacked: enthusiastic input from our area's regional transportation planning organization, the Genesee Transportation Council (GTC). In early 2018, a GTC staff member attended the annual meeting of the Transportation Research Board in Washington, DC, where one session described the many-hours-long traffic jams caused by unpreparedness for the 2017 eclipse. The lessons presented in that session made Jim Stack, GTC's executive director, and his colleague Lori Maher, the program manager for community engagement, realize that our area could avoid the issues that plagued our nation's highways and smaller roads in 2017 if we planned well in advance of the 2024 eclipse. I later discovered that involving traffic and emergency-management entities was a common difficulty among eclipse community organizers in other regions, but Jim and Lori had us covered right from the start.

In April 2019, almost exactly five years before the 2024 eclipse, the RMSC hosted astronomy educator Janet Ivey-Duensing for two days of eclipse preparation seminars in Rochester, which were attended by over 150 stakeholders. Janet, founder of the PBS program *Janet's Planet*, brought valuable strategies from her experiences assisting Nashville, Tennessee and Columbia, South Carolina with their 2017 eclipse preparations, which allowed us to avoid creating our plans from scratch. She also connected us with leaders of the American Astronomical Society's (AAS) Solar Eclipse Task Force (SETF). That summer, the RMSC's President and CEO, Hillary Olson, and I attended the SETF's conference, where I met key national leaders, including Dr. Rick Feinberg and Dr. Angela Speck, who had been guiding the AAS's eclipse efforts since 2014. These national connections greatly enhanced Rochester's access to the resources, expertise, and energy of the people in that network—many of whom you'll meet in the upcoming chapters—further positioning us for success.

We had everything we needed. And yet, most people who heard us talk thought we were crazy. "Hundreds of people are preparing for something that's not going to happen for five years?" they'd say. "Who knows what will happen between now and then?"

We found out soon enough what would happen: Less than a year after Janet gave us her playbook and we started making connections outside our area, the world shut down. In other regions, the COVID-19 pandemic thwarted early eclipse planning, but Rochester's momentum couldn't be stopped.

Plus, we had Dan.

The first official meeting of the Rochester Eclipse Task Force had convened on a beautiful fall day in October of 2019 on the campus of the RMSC, right next door to where everything had started back in 2012. Artist and astronomer Dr. Tyler Nordgren, whose 2017 poster art series had recently been acquired by the Smithsonian Institution for its permanent collection (and who designed the cover of this book), was at the podium in front of a crowd of several dozen Rochesterians, recounting how the professional astronomy community had helped prepare regions in the path of totality in 2017. In the front row was 29-year-old Dan Schneiderman, gripping his personal copy of Tyler's book *Sun Moon Earth: The History of Solar Eclipses from Omens of Doom to Einstein and Exoplanets,*[1] and—as Dan himself would say later—"asking too many questions and offering too many ideas" about how Rochester could best take advantage of its position in the path of totality of the upcoming 2024 eclipse.

I was standing at the side of the stage next to Hillary. She leaned toward me, angled her chin toward Dan, and whispered, "See that guy? That's who's going to manage the RMSC's eclipse efforts. He's perfect."

In March of 2021, Hillary fulfilled her 2019 vow to hire Dan as the RMSC's eclipse partnership coordinator; in October of 2022, the position became full-time. By April 2024, Dan's work on the eclipse had helped raise $361,000 in grants and sponsorships (and $565,000 overall); he had given hundreds

---

[1] Tyler Nordgren, *Sun, Moon, Earth: The History of Solar Eclipses from Omens of Doom to Einstein and Exoplanets,* Basic Books, 2016.

of science education and safety presentations, and he had met with thousands of people at festivals and other gatherings, usually accompanied by one of the six pairs of the 205-pound giant eclipse glasses he had specially commissioned.[2]

During the following years leading up to April 2024, Dan and I became known around Rochester as the eclipse nerds whose energy and enthusiasm never wavered. We ran monthly stakeholder meetings, we presented at libraries, Rotary meetings, schools, social clubs, and neighboring tourism bureaus. We appeared in countless segments on local TV, radio, and podcasts to spread the word about what would happen and why everyone should make sure that on the afternoon of April 8, they would be squarely in the path of totality. And Dan set up and disassembled those glasses more times than was probably healthy for his back.

So Rochester not only had the perfect catalyst but also the perfect group of people who recognized its potential to have a profoundly positive impact on our region.

The Rochester Eclipse Task Force eventually attracted over 750 members from a wide variety of sectors, almost 200 of whom were highly engaged. We had sector members from tourism, government, education, community management, emergency management, arts, culture, and commerce. We had experts in accessibility and inclusion, traffic predictions, and outreach to every corner of our area. We were unified in our identity as the United States region most prepared for the eclipse.

In short, it worked. In fact, it worked not just for Rochester but for the whole country: We became nationally recognized as

---

[2] TheEclipseEffect.com has photos of the giant eclipse glasses.

the leader in eclipse preparations. After the AAS's SETF met in Rochester in 2022, Rick asked me to co-chair the national task force with Angela so I could help them help other communities in the 2024 path prepare as Rochester had done. This gave me unprecedented access to the people throughout North America and the rest of the world who were as determined as I was to help ensure that no one missed the opportunity to learn about the eclipse and experience it safely. I also finally had a community where no one thought I was crazy.

Serving as national co-chair also connected me with science journalist Jamie Carter, the co-author of this book. Jamie writes for Forbes.com, Space.com, *Sky & Telescope*, and *Travel+Leisure*; he also runs WhenIsTheNextEclipse.com. Jamie wrote hundreds of articles in the years leading up to the 2024 eclipse, including several that featured me and Ella. Jamie's Rolodex of contacts, his archive of dozens of interviews, and his twenty-five years telling the stories behind science make him the perfect storyteller for this effort. He's also just a great guy, and, now, he's the exclamation point at the end of my personal eclipse story.

As Jamie and I interacted with all of the people in the communities making it happen, it became clear that each, in their own way, was an example of what we have come to call the Eclipse Effect.

The Eclipse Effect describes how ordinary people can harness extraordinary moments to create something remarkable and lasting by uniting diverse talents and communities. At its core, the Eclipse Effect begins with a catalyst—an event so compelling it captures attention and ignites curiosity in a small group of visionaries who see its potential for creating value in the world. By harnessing the catalyst's momentum and deliberately uniting people to work together, they can best take advantage of that moment. Ultimately, the true power of the Eclipse Effect lies in the lasting impact it leaves behind: an enduring legacy that extends far beyond the event itself.

This book offers a framework for turning any catalyst—a natural event, milestone, or unique opportunity—into a lasting legacy. It is applicable to regions large and small, to businesses, to schools, nonprofit boards, and even to families. By emphasizing vision, collaboration, and strategic action, it provides a road map for uniting diverse talents and communities to maximize potential and create meaningful, long-term impact in virtually any context.

In a world frequently overshadowed by division and uncertainty, this approach inspires hope, promotes unity, and reinforces the belief that meaningful change is possible through collaboration. Leveraging Eclipse Effect strategies allows individuals and communities to reclaim a sense of agency during a time when many feel overwhelmed or disillusioned by larger societal forces. By seeking and leveraging extraordinary catalysts with clear vision, collaboration, and action, ordinary people can create significant, positive change.

That's why we thought it deserved a book.

This book explores the core elements of the Eclipse Effect and demonstrates their relevance to various efforts and communities, set against the compelling stories of the 2017 and 2024 North American eclipses. We argue that seizing these opportunities to build strong, inclusive communities is essential, and we demonstrate the transformative power of such efforts. By drawing from real-life examples, we show how to recognize and embrace catalysts as opportunities to foster connection, collaboration, and lasting impact. Readers will be introduced to an inspiring cast of individuals—Angela Speck, Rick Fienberg, Dan Schneiderman, Trish Erzfeld, Sarah Wolfe, and many others—who have brought the Eclipse Effect to life in meaningful ways, from grand-scale initiatives to local grassroots efforts. Along the way, the book provides practical guidance for creating and sustaining communities: rallying others around a shared vision, building a cohesive identity, keeping the group motivated, measuring success, and ensuring a lasting legacy. It's both a call to action and a guide for turning these moments into remarkable, enduring achievements.

The book also describes how to define success in ways potential leaders might not have considered, and it provides ideas for managing the inevitable failures and disappointments while creating communities that last...because no matter how many contingencies we anticipate or how carefully we prepare, there will be things we can't control.

Although many communities in the path of totality had gloriously clear skies that made for perfect eclipse viewing, when Rochester's moment finally arrived at 3:20 p.m. on April 8, 2024, we had thick clouds. That meant that our skies got deeply, profoundly dark, which was a beautiful experience... but we missed what others in the country saw—the "hole in the sky."

"If anyone deserved to see the Sun that day, it was Rochester," many people who knew of our countless hours of preparation have told me.

"That's okay," I always respond. "Our magic happened on the ground."

—*Debra Ross, February 2025*

CHAPTER 1

The Eclipse Effect

Dallas–Fort Worth doesn't just dream big. Home to 6.5 million people, the region has 23 Fortune 500 companies and a can-do spirit as vast as its highways. When Dallasites set their sights on something, it's usually a slam dunk. But when it came to the rare opportunity to position this vast metroplex as the premier destination for a rare total solar eclipse, the stars didn't align.

"We assumed the Dallas–Fort Worth area would naturally come together in full force for this rare event," says Jo Trizila, founder and CEO of TrizCom PR & Pitch PR, who set up Total Eclipse DFW to focus efforts to promote the region's efforts. "That wasn't the case."

That's despite the celestial geography being very kind to Dallas–Fort Worth. "Almost every city in the region was touched by totality—and we have over 300 cities," says Trizila. "Each city wanted to do their own thing and stay on their own sides, and they didn't work together."

Dallas started preparing for the eclipse way too late. Trizila didn't even know what a total solar eclipse was before she started Total Eclipse DFW in the summer of 2023, but she could see there was a need for information. Being late meant problems sourcing enough solar eclipse glasses for local schools, with Chinese New Year in February unexpectedly causing major supply chain issues. Its glasses weren't delivered until March, which left little time for distribution.

But Trizila was right: There *was* a thirst for information. Her TotalEclipseDFW.com website got over 100,000 visitors, mostly from organic keywords, and was linked to in over 400 news articles. There was a particularly large demand for information about the eclipse from the Hispanic community. "Out of every phone call we got, every other one was a Spanish speaker wanting something," says Trizila, who couldn't keep up with the demand for merchandise. With more time, affiliate marketing schemes and drop-shipping would have helped meet demand. "It would have saved a lot of us a lot of legwork of having to create things from scratch," says Trizila.

In the end, Dallas brought in $700 million in revenue from the eclipse, but it could have been a lot more. "If we had acted together, it could have been in the billions—Dallas missed a huge opportunity," says Trizila.

On April 8, 2024, the clouds parted, and most Dallasites got a clear view of totality, but it wasn't the event it could have been.

What Dallas had missed out on was the Eclipse Effect.

In 2000, Robert D. Putnam published *Bowling Alone: The Collapse and Revival of American Community*, a groundbreaking examination of the decline of community life in the United States during the latter half of the twentieth century. Putnam argues that this decline was driven largely by the erosion of social capital—the networks of relationships that build trust, cooperation, and mutual benefit. The book ignited widespread debate about the role of social connections in modern life, shaping public policy, urban planning, and community development research in the years following its release. More than two decades later, its arguments remain relevant, and its influence remains significant.

Putnam divides social capital into two types:

- Bonding social capital, which exists within tight-knit, homogenous groups. These communities form naturally—examples are religious congregations, friend circles, and cultural groups—and provide support and identity for their members.

- Bridging social capital, which connects people across diverse lines. Building bridging communities requires deliberate effort but fosters innovation and broad impact.

In *Bowling Alone*, different types of networks rely on different types of social capital:

> Some forms of social capital are, by choice or necessity, inward-looking and tend to reinforce exclusive identities and homogeneous groups. Examples of bonding social capital include ethnic fraternal organizations, church-based women's reading groups, and fashionable country clubs. Other networks are outward-looking and encompass people across diverse social cleavages. Examples of bridging social capital include the civil rights movement, many youth service groups, and ecumenical religious organizations.[3]

Putnam regards the different types of social capital simply as facts about how humans act. One is not superior to the other; rather, both are necessary for the health of society.

> Bonding social capital is good for undergirding specific reciprocity and mobilizing solidarity. Dense networks in ethnic enclaves, for example, provide crucial social and psychological support for less fortunate members of the community, while furnishing start-up financing, markets, and reliable labor for local entrepreneurs. Bridging

---

[3] Robert D. Putnam, *Bowling Alone: The Collapse and Revival of American Community*, Simon & Schuster, 2000, 22.

networks, by contrast, are better for linkage to external assets and for information distribution... Bridging social capital can generate broader identities and reciprocity, whereas bonding social capital bolsters our narrower selves.... Bonding social capital constitutes a kind of sociological superglue, whereas bridging social capital provides a sociological WD-40.[4]

The Need for Bridging Communities

Putnam's concept of bonding social capital suggests that bonded networks emerge organically, driven by shared interests, backgrounds, and attitudes. In contrast, communities built through bridging social capital require intentional effort and energy to unite people across divides.

In today's polarized cultural landscape, where individuals often retreat into "safe" bonded groups, the challenge of creating bridging communities grows ever more daunting. "In America ... we never all do the same thing at the same time," says Kristopher Harsh, a member of the Cleveland City Council who worked on the city's 2024 eclipse preparations. "We don't watch the same TV shows or listen to the same music. We don't eat the same foods, and the one time a year when we do—Thanksgiving—we intentionally avoid everyone except our immediate families."

Creating a purposeful community whose members represent widely differing ideals, areas of expertise, and skills is no trivial task, and it can feel easier to stop before even starting. So it often takes an external catalyst—a positive opportunity

---

[4]   Putnam, *Bowling Alone*, 22-23.

like an eclipse or an emergency like a natural disaster—to spark the motivation to overcome barriers that might otherwise seem too high to scale. Visionary leaders play a crucial role in seizing these moments and rallying others to recognize their potential and contribute their strengths.

"The current climate in the US is so deeply divisive and dis-spirited that the phenomenon of a total eclipse drawing tens of millions of people together—of all races, religions, political persuasions, economic statuses—seemed like a necessary tonic to remind us all about community, perspective and our profound interdependence, once we see ourselves in cosmic perspective," says David Heilbroner, the filmmaker who conceived the documentary *Totality*, which showcases how the 2024 eclipse preparations transformed communities and the people within them.

Diversity and Inclusion: Keys to Bridging Communities

Why is diversity so valuable in forming a strong bridging community? In short, it's because no one can know everything, think of everything, or do everything, especially in a volunteer effort. Communities whose leaders can attract members with diverse skills, perspectives, resources, and networks—and who can inspire those members to contribute their ideas and energy—can address complex challenges that no homogeneous group can tackle alone.

Trish Erzfeld, director of Perry County Heritage Tourism in Perryville, Missouri, happened to reside at the "eclipse crossroads" where the 2017 and 2024 paths of totality intersected.[5] After successfully leading Perry County's 2017 eclipse efforts, she was tapped to chair Missouri's statewide task force for the 2024 eclipse while simultaneously preparing her region for its "Back in Black" themed reprise. Erzfeld emphasizes that successful efforts rely on inspiring individuals and small communities to take the initiative rather than depending solely on large organizations or government authorities. Equally important, she believes leaders must see themselves as equal participants in the planning process rather than seeking visibility or acclaim—a mindset she acknowledges is neither easy nor common.

"Collaboration is an elusive word in community planning," Erzfeld explains. "Everyone knows they need it to achieve great things, but few are willing to give up recognition to reach it."

However, when leaders set aside personal interests and prioritize engaging diverse participants, communities can unlock more effective collaboration. This approach allows everyone to draw on the varied experiences, perspectives, and resources individuals bring to the effort, resulting in stronger outcomes with greater impact.

Rather than paying lip service to the concept of "diversity," wise community organizers recognize that the strength of this kind of community is rooted in the differences in perspectives, backgrounds, and networks of the individuals within it. When people feel valued for what they uniquely bring to a table, they are more likely to invest in collective efforts; such a dynamic creates an environment where communities flourish, generating meaningful change that benefits both individuals and the

---

[5]   The odds of any one location experiencing two total solar eclipses just seven
     years apart is about 1 in 5,600. —*Jamie*

broader society. These moments not only create collaboration but also foster a shared sense of identity—an "us-ness"—that bonds people together and provides lasting value long after the catalyst has passed.

So people looking to enact change in the world should first look for catalysts, and when they recognize such gifts from the universe, they should make the most of the opportunities they present.

The Eclipse Effect

What we call the Eclipse Effect is the phenomenon in which a temporary network formed in response to a unique opportunity transitions, through exceptional coordination and leadership, into a permanent new community of people of widely diverse backgrounds, skills, and resources. It has four main components:

1. The catalyst or extraordinary event that sparks people's interest and attention
2. The vision and foresight required to see the potential in that event
3. The deliberate effort to bring diverse communities and talents together to maximize the opportunity
4. The lasting impact and resonance that extend beyond the initial catalyst

A total solar eclipse is vanishingly rare for any specific location, occurring in the same spot only once every 366 years, on average.[6] "Experiencing totality is uniquely powerful,

---

[6] Ernie Wright, Laurence Schuler, and Ian Jones, "5,000 Years of Total Solar Eclipses, Total Solar Eclipse: April 8, 2024," NASA's Scientific Visualization Studio.

transforming day into night and revealing the Sun's corona," says Dr. Rick Fienberg, the project manager of the American Astronomical Society's Solar Eclipse Task Force. "It's a sight far more awe-inspiring than even a 99% partial solar eclipse."

Awe is central to the total solar eclipse experience. "I've seen three total solar eclipses and cried my eyes out every time," says Sævar Helgi Bragason, an astronomy and science communicator in Iceland who's been preparing since 2015 for his country's total solar eclipse in 2026 — its first since 1954. "The last one I traveled to see was filmed and broadcast on primetime TV as part of a science show I host, so everyone in Iceland saw me crying," he says. "People started to appreciate what I'm always saying about a total solar eclipse being something everyone should experience."

Dr. Kate Russo, a clinical psychologist and renowned eclipse expert, who has helped communities around the world coordinate eclipse planning for over a decade, believes that the opportunity to experience something profound is a powerful catalyst for community and stakeholder engagement. "The promise of a shared awe experience is that initial catalyst, and the immovable deadline sparks people into action," she says. "But community leaders need to tap into something deeper and longer-lasting— the desire to build community identity and legacy beyond the fleeting moment of totality. Individual motivations and values are the drivers of building a strong community network with a common goal. Then the shared collective experience of totality and profound awe creates that long-tail effect that, if nurtured, can continue these community bonds. But here's the thing—you don't have to wait for an eclipse. Any community can achieve remarkable things when its members share the will, desire, and determination to collaborate for the greater good.

This emphasis on collaboration can inspire and motivate communities to work together towards a common goal."

The ideal catalyst varies by circumstance; it needn't be a dramatic natural phenomenon like an eclipse. It could be a planned event, such as the Olympics or the Super Bowl, or a milestone such as the two hundred and fiftieth anniversary of the signing of the United States Declaration of Independence in 2026. In business, it can be the sudden emergence of a new technology—such as artificial intelligence—that can spur people to imagine new efficiencies of scale, new products, or whole new industries. In families, the catalyst can be a significant milestone, like a couple's fiftieth wedding anniversary or the birth of a child, or the relocation for a new job. Catalysts can also arise from negative events, such as natural disasters, riots, or wars. What defines them as catalysts is recognizing their potential to inspire collective action—harnessing their inherent momentum to bring people together and drive the world toward positive change.

The total solar eclipse on August 21, 2017, nicknamed the "Great American Eclipse," united millions in shared awe under the path of totality. The experience was not only widely anticipated—there had not been a major eclipse in the United States since 1979—but well-attended and widely broadcast. The experience dissolved barriers, inspiring countless organizers and communities to come together to make the event accessible and meaningful for all. As the vivid images and accounts dominated the internet for weeks afterward, there was much discussion of how the next major North American eclipse was only seven years later. Many recognized the opportunity for their regions to make the most of the upcoming experience and started organizing years in advance.

Harsh, who introduced a resolution to Cleveland declaring April 8, 2024, as "CLEclipse Day," noted that the eclipse was a rare chance for communities to come together and experience something as one. "This is the first time in most of our lives that we all did the same thing at the same time and had the same experience: pure awe in the face of nature," he says. "Everyone felt it. Everyone knew it. Everyone is better because of it."

Rochester, New York organized as a unified front, marketing itself as the destination for eclipse watchers. "Rochester gets a gold star—it stands out as a great example of a city that takes a championing approach," says Russo. "The city found their unique way, unique strategy, and went for it—from its branding and social media to its executive team and how they built its extensive network. They saw opportunity after opportunity and just went for it. They were amazing." The result: Rochester drew massive attention and economic activity, proving that collaboration could be as or more powerful than financial resources.

In contrast, the state of Texas—even with its reputation for doing everything bigger—failed to capitalize on the eclipse as smaller regions had done. Many areas in the sprawling Texas metroplex of Dallas–Fort Worth, and the cities between and beyond, had small pockets of local organizers. But instead of building something bigger together, they stayed focused on their corners. "Every city organized its events but only publicized them locally," says Trizila. "It felt like they were competing to attract eclipse traffic, even though there was plenty of opportunity to share across the metroplex."

Eclipse collaboration across the Lone Star State was hard to find. "There was a reluctance to pool resources for regional promotion," says Trizila. "A stronger regional effort—starting earlier—could have presented DFW as the premier destination

JAMIE CARTER & DEBRA ROSS

within the path of totality. But DFW and, for that matter, Texas, lost out on national visibility, the number of eclipse visitors, and economic activity."

For all its glittering office towers, business brilliance, and cowboy grit, Dallas–Fort Worth was reminded that sometimes even the most successful places can get stuck in their silos and miss their moment to shine. It stands as a lesson in the challenges of unity.

The connections established within bridging communities often evolve into enduring, personally rewarding bonds for participants. Debbie Ferrell was one of the original organizers of the "Embrace the Dark 2024" eclipse celebration in Geneva, New York; she worked for more than a year before the eclipse to unite her community in the effort. It had long-lasting consequences: "This entire program led to business collaborations, formation of new relationships and strengthening of bonds within the smaller neighborhoods in our community," she says. "I have been invited to meetings with the city, county and state, and have many new contacts and go-to people for new endeavors."

Leadership in Bridging Communities

Leadership is often envisioned in a traditional sense, like the Pied Piper of Hamelin: a singular figure wielding power and influence to command attention and compel action. The Piper uses his music to compel the attention and obedience of the rats and, later, the children of Hamelin; he exerts control through his unique ability and expects compliance with his plan. This book challenges the idea that leadership requires power or authority to achieve results. We regard effective leadership as being about building bridges between people rather than exercising control or issuing directives from the top. A successful leader's primary role is to create structures and systems that bind the community together, fostering collaboration and mutual support.

In a bridging community, leadership doesn't depend on charisma or a rigid plan for others to follow. Instead, your job is to connect with members on a personal level: discovering who they are, why they're involved, and what unique skills they bring to the table. By celebrating these contributions, you cultivate an environment where members feel valued and motivated to contribute their best. This kind of leadership requires self-motivation, adaptability, emotional intelligence, and a deep commitment to helping others develop their talents. It also involves resisting the temptation to control outcomes or assert authority. Instead, you focus on building trust and a shared sense of purpose, creating an atmosphere where individuals can align their efforts toward the collective goal. In doing so, you enable the community to thrive through connection, collaboration, and shared vision.

Managing a community that inspires both individual and collective success while fostering personal fulfillment is challenging but straightforward. Each member joins the effort for their own reasons, and effective leaders take the time to understand these motivations. By keeping them in mind, leaders can provide the tools and connections members need to pursue their individual goals within the broader initiative—ensuring they feel happy, inspired, and supported throughout the process.

Therefore, the leadership style needed for bridging communities stands apart from traditional models. Leaders in these settings might be recognized as authorities or passionate individuals, but their primary role is to facilitate connections and foster collaboration, not to command. They realize, and celebrate, the fact that the leaders have no power to make anyone do anything; they can only create a circumstance in which it is worthwhile and fun to do so. They define success in ways that adapt as the effort evolves, maintaining focus on a shared, flexible vision. Along the way, they celebrate milestones to keep the community motivated, and they devise strategies to ensure a lasting legacy, preserving the value of individual and collective achievements and the lessons learned throughout the process.

Effective leaders in bridging communities play three critical roles:

- Glue: keeping the group united and cohesive
- Cheerleader: motivating members and celebrating progress at every stage
- Architect: providing the tools, setting goals, and ensuring inclusivity for all participants

This facilitative leadership style empowers members to take ownership of the community's mission, fostering a shared sense of purpose and identity. As we move forward in this book, we will delve into the practical steps of creating bridging communities:

- Identifying who should lead
- Developing strategies to sustain connection
- Overcoming challenges
- Celebrating milestones
- Crafting a shared vision for the future

From Bridging to Bonding

"With community comes identity," says Jimmy Wales, founder of Wikipedia, in his book *The Seven Rules of Trust*.[7] But that outcome isn't automatic. A bridging community—initially held together by a few leaders and a shared event—only evolves into a bonded one when nurtured with care and intention. Over time, its members develop a lasting sense of identity shaped by common history and purpose. That identity becomes the glue that holds the community together long after the original catalyst has faded. Bridging communities have the potential to be a transformative force for societal resilience: Whether formed under the fleeting shadow of a total solar eclipse or in response to other challenges or opportunities, the principles of bridging, leadership, and legacy remain the same. Even if a community's stated goals are not fully achieved, the networks they create and the individuals they empower can drive future efforts that bring new value. The full story of any such effort includes the growth and strengthening of the network, its ability to inspire future collaborations and the personal fulfillment and empowerment of its members. This dual impact—collective and individual—highlights the critical role of bridging communities in fostering innovation, connection, and hope for a healthier, more inclusive world.

This is the Eclipse Effect.

---

[7] Jimmy Wales, *The Seven Rules of Trust: A Blueprint for Building Things That Last*, Crown Currency, 2025, 63.

CHAPTER 2

Deciding to Lead

When an eerie dusk fell suddenly around him at 11:09 a.m. as he stood on the deck of the *MS Zaandam* cruise ship near Mazatlán, Mexico, a decade of intense work by Dr. Rick Fienberg silently sunsetted. In the midmorning twilight, he lowered his solar filters, placed them in a shirt pocket, and looked up to see the Sun's delicate, whitish corona appear before his naked eyes. It was his fifteenth total solar eclipse.

Thousands of miles to the northeast, about 50 million North Americans were safely viewing the dangerous partial stages of the eclipse through solar filters that mostly met rigorous international safety standards. Few knew of Fienberg's herculean effort to keep a continent of people's eyes safe.

A professional astronomer, educator, and author, Fienberg first maintained a verified list of approved solar filter glasses suppliers before the 2017 eclipse, when he was the American Astronomical Society's (AAS) press officer. He painstakingly vetted a list of International Organization for Standardization (ISO)–compliant manufacturers that, thanks to its promotion by NASA, became the most-visited page in the history of the AAS. It was the primary defense North Americans had against manufacturers who tried to flood the market with counterfeit eclipse glasses in the weeks and months leading up to the eclipse.

"I thought I was doing a favor to the community, but it became maddening," says Fienberg. Fake glasses infiltrated online platforms, vendors bribed and manipulated for a spot on his list, and online sales platforms inconsistently enforced safety standards. "The marketplace is out of control," he says, recounting his endless hours verifying lab reports and fielding panicked calls from vendors. Even after he boarded the *MS Zaandam*, Fienberg continued to deal with crises, uncovering fraudulent products and issuing last-minute warnings.

Fienberg's work paid off despite the stress and chaos, with minimal eye injuries reported. But looking ahead to the next eclipses worldwide—in Europe in 2026, Africa in 2027, and Australia in 2028—as well as the next ones in North America in the 2040s—he urges the industry to require manufacturers to maintain their own verified lists to ease the burden on future efforts, although he acknowledges the difficulties that would involve. "I wouldn't wish what I went through on anyone," he says, reflecting on a decade of vigilance, perseverance, and service.

Fienberg, who uniquely recognized and filled a critical gap in eclipse preparations, will never hear a thank-you from the millions whose vision he helped safeguard. Fienberg's dedication exemplifies the quiet, transformative leadership that asks not for gratitude but simply, "If not me, who?"

Bridging communities that are created as a mechanism for change tend to have leaders who are there for one of three reasons:

1. A sudden catalyst causes people to see potential and become leaders.

   A catalyst suddenly presents itself, causing the soon-to-be leaders to recognize it as an opportunity to effect change; they see how to capitalize on its momentum and take the leap to lead the effort.

2. People whose job or profession it is to enact a certain kind of change in the world decide to pull a community together to do so.

   These leaders already hold a professional role or career dedicated to positive change and look for opportunities to pull together a community to help them.

3. People who want to lead for change find a reason to do it.

   These leaders are people who are alert to opportunities that align with their ideals or missions. When opportune moments arise to pull together a community of people who share their goals, they seize it.

Communities managing the recent North American eclipses were largely led by people in categories one and two: people who were catalyzed into a passion for the cause, and people whose jobs it is to be galvanized to action. This book's co-authors fit squarely into category one, but they're not alone.

"I live and breathe eclipses," says Dr. Kate Russo, an author, psychologist, and eclipse chaser who is also the founder of Being in The Shadow and a member of the American Astronomical Society (AAS) Solar Eclipse Task Force (SETF). "The total solar eclipse is a life experience, not just a quick fleeting event. Totality happens above you, around you, and within you."

Russo became captivated by total solar eclipses after experiencing her first in 1999. Over time, she turned her fascination into action, researching and sharing the totality experience, and then further by helping communities in upcoming paths of totality prepare to make the most of the rare opportunity.

"I champion eclipse coordinators on the ground because they usually haven't experienced totality before, but must share the experience with others. It's difficult enough to do in soundbites, let alone if you haven't yet experienced one before," she says. Russo's influential publication, "White Paper on Community Solar Eclipse Planning," became an essential resource for communities preparing for the 2024 event.[8]

Dan McGlaun, an Indiana-based eclipse enthusiast, also saw the potential of eclipses to catalyze learning and community engagement. A veteran of nine total solar eclipses, McGlaun created Eclipse2024.org as a comprehensive resource for the public, including an innovative simulator showing what the eclipse would look like from any location.[9] He also gave presentations to dozens of local groups and helped towns in Indiana promote eclipse tourism. "The Midwest is always called 'flyover country,' and we don't get an opportunity to be in the spotlight very often," McGlaun notes. "But I also wanted to evangelize eclipses: How better to feel a connection to the universe than participating in an alignment of Earth, the Moon, and the Sun?"

For others, leadership emerges naturally from their professional roles. Trish Erzfeld was a former truck driver; when she became tourism director of Perry County, she leveraged her community's good fortune of being positioned in the "eclipse crossroads" of the 2017 and 2024 eclipse paths. It was a twice-in-a-lifetime chance to highlight her region. "I wasn't the most knowledgeable person at first," she admits, "but I had a vision of what this could mean for our community."

Erzfeld rallied businesses, civic groups, and residents to prepare for the events, helping Perryville attract thousands of visitors. She spearheaded a three-day "SolarFest" celebration for each eclipse; in 2017, the event temporarily doubled the population of her city from 8,500 to 17,500. By 2024, she had

---

[8]   Kate Russo, "White Paper: Community Eclipse Planning, Being in the Shadow," September 2015.
[9]   Eclipse2024.org.

become a key figure in national eclipse planning as chair of the Missouri Eclipse Task Force and a prominent member of the AAS SETF working groups. "I wanted people to understand that this was more than just an event—it was an investment in our town's future," she says. Only seven short years later, Perryville's SolarFest 2024 attracted over 56,000 visitors to the area, almost seven times the 2017 visitors.

Dr. Angela Speck found leadership through her dual passions for astronomy and education. As co-chair of the AAS SETF, Speck worked tirelessly to raise awareness of eclipses, blending her professional expertise with her personal mission to make astronomy accessible to the public. Her involvement in advance of the 2017 eclipse began as early as 2014 and has since solidified her reputation as a leader in eclipse education and planning.

This book is relevant to leaders and aspiring leaders, regardless of why you find yourself drawn to leadership. Still, it is particularly aimed at those in category two—whose job is to lead and seek strategies—and in category three, for those who feel deeply that the world needs transformative change and think they might be in a position to help make it happen. You may not see yourself as a natural leader, and taking on this work might feel daunting. The good news is that there are proven strategies to empower leaders—both established and emerging—to inspire, guide, and nurture the kinds of diverse communities capable of driving positive change.

How to Be the Glue

One of the leader's main functions is as the "glue" holding a community together as its members achieve their goals individually and collectively. Building and maintaining bridges carefully and deliberately between people who might not ordinarily know or work with each other requires sustained effort: Brainstorming about who should connect, and then making that happen through repeated emails, phone calls, and in-person introductions. If a leader is genuine and approachable, that's helpful, of course—after all, people who like you are usually willing to be connected with others who like you. But success in building strong bridges between people requires something more fundamental: trust. And trust, as Jimmy Wales says in *The Seven Rules of Trust*, is fundamentally practical, not emotional.

> We don't trust people in the abstract. We trust people to *do* something. (Or not do something, as the case may be.) When your car breaks down, you leave it with a mechanic you trust, meaning a mechanic you are confident will make the car run again and bill you honestly and fairly. When you say you trust a colleague's judgment, you mean you think your colleague can and will choose the best way to achieve a goal.[10]

So earning the trust of those you want to attract to your mission is critical. "Make it personal, and scale up," Wales advises.[11] Leaders who do this most successfully cultivate the following personality traits:

1. Servant leadership/anti-authority orientation

---

[10] Jimmy Wales, *The Seven Rules of Trust: A Blueprint for Building Things That Last,* Crown Currency, 2025, 29.
[11] Wales, *The Seven Rules of Trust,* 35.

2. Clear purpose
3. Fact orientation
4. People orientation/cultural sensitivity
5. Emotional intelligence and stability
6. Flexibility and strategic agility

1. Servant leadership/anti-authority orientation

The cornerstone of a thriving bridging community is servant leadership.

Unlike traditional hierarchical authority, servant leadership emphasizes empowering others and fostering collaboration. Leaders in such communities exist not to command but to nurture the group's health and cohesion. They wield no inherent power and actively communicate their role as facilitators, not rulers. A servant leader supports the community by offering tools, guidance, and inspiration, helping to advance shared goals through vision and ideas that resonate with and inspire others. They recognize that their position is not one in which they tell people what to do, they can only inspire people to want to work together toward a shared vision, in whatever way they decide is best.

"Leadership means facilitating rather than directing," explains Speck, who, throughout her professional career as an astrophysicist has cultivated a leadership style that enables the people around her to be their best selves. As co-chair of the AAS SETF, she instinctively understood that success in galvanizing awareness of the upcoming eclipses was only possible by tapping dozens of others who shared her vision and creating a structure that benefited their own work as well as that of the

SETF. "At every layer, we had working groups doing their own things. We deputized others."

By structuring a community in which people's own interests align with the collective interest, all of the individual achievements can be celebrated as contributing to the goal of the community, and the leaders of such an organization can properly take pride in the achievements of everyone within it. "People would ask me why I was working so hard for two minutes and forty seconds [of totality], but it's not really the minutes and seconds we're working for—it's the lifetimes that we inspire," says Erzfeld. Inasmuch as anyone owns the work they do, leaders who have helped their community members make connections within and outside the community can take psychological ownership of the future value that those growing bonds will generate, even if they never experience them directly.

All of the above is a long way of saying that if you think leadership is about personal power and recognition for your work, you need to reorganize that thinking if you want to be effective.

2. Clear purpose

"Clear purpose" is Rule Number Three in Wales' Seven Rules. "A strong, clear, positive purpose is essential for people to work together and make something wonderful," he says.[12] A well-defined vision helps set the stage for success, but aligning around it can be challenging when people bring a range of goals and priorities to the table. There are two key aspects to purpose in leadership: defining your own purpose in leading

---

[12] Wales, *The Seven Rules of Trust,* 49.

the community and clearly articulating the broader purpose or impact you want the community to achieve.

First, you must understand your personal purpose—why you are stepping into a leadership role and what you hope to accomplish. This clarity helps you set realistic, achievable goals that align with your own mission. It also keeps you focused and grounded, providing the internal motivation needed to lead effectively, especially when challenges arise.

Second, it's crucial to communicate a shared purpose to the community, framing the overall vision in a way that inspires and engages. This purpose must be broad enough to encompass the diverse contributions and successes of the members, yet specific enough to provide clear direction. This balance ensures cohesiveness without becoming overly prescriptive or dictatorial.

For some leaders, what they experienced in the aftermath of the previous United States eclipse in 2017 focused their entire approach to the eclipse in 2024. Sarah Wolfe, an eclipse coordinator in Vincennes, Indiana, shared how the memory of trying to get home after the 2017 event profoundly influenced her planning for her area for 2024. "There were cars everywhere. Gas stations had closed out of lack of inventory or sheer exhaustion. Route 1 was a parking lot," she says. The logistical chaos was a stark reminder of the scale of the event and the strain it could place on small communities. "A two-hour drive stretched into an eight-hour fever dream," says Wolfe. "Upon applying for the position of eclipse director, this was the scene that had dropped in my mind."

For leaders like Wolfe, these reflections weren't just cautionary tales—they became a catalyst for proactive, community-focused planning. The logistical chaos of 2017 highlighted the critical need to address transportation, infrastructure, and visitor management well in advance to prevent a repeat of the overwhelming strain on small communities. However, Wolfe and others recognized that solving such complex challenges couldn't be achieved through top-down directives or a one-size-fits-all approach.

Instead, their strategy centered on collaboration and empowerment. Leaders identified key areas likely to be affected—such as traffic flow, resource availability, and emergency response—and brought together community members with expertise in these fields. By providing these experts with the resources, autonomy, and support needed to develop solutions, they fostered an environment of collective problem-solving. This approach not only ensured practical and locally tailored remedies but also strengthened the community's sense of ownership and preparedness ahead of the 2024 eclipse.

Effective leaders avoid narrowly defining the community's goals, which risks excluding valuable contributions that might not fit a rigid mold. Instead, they adopt what might be called the "some but any" principle: The purpose is defined enough to unify the group but abstract enough to allow for multiple paths to success. This flexibility ensures that any action supporting the shared purpose is celebrated as a success, encouraging creativity and ownership among members.

Being transparent about what you're doing can be helpful, particularly if you're daunted at the sheer size of a task or an event. "I always said I wanted my community to have an awesome eclipse experience," says Erzfeld. "I did not say the 50,000 eclipse visitors coming to Perryville will have an awesome experience." She worked on the assumption that visitors want an authentic experience just like the locals, calculating that many benefits of the effort to do that, and only that, would naturally flow from there. "We planned an awesome experience for the local community that would build relationships, grow local ambassadors, attract visitors, who will have an awesome experience, and economic impact will naturally happen," says Erzfeld. "If you play your cards right, in the years to come, new visitors, new businesses and new opportunities will follow."

There is no clearer purpose than protecting the eyesight of millions of Americans, but for Fienberg, that meant rubbing shoulders with manufacturers and resellers whose only wish was profit. Linked to by NASA, his personally vetted list of suppliers of safe solar viewers and filters became a badge of quality and assurance in an out-of-control marketplace of resellers and overseas manufacturers. Some vied to get their occasionally counterfeit or unverified products rubber-stamped or placed higher on the list. "It's not just difficult or challenging or time-consuming, it's maddening, especially when you get people starting to offer you bribes," says Fienberg.[13] "I didn't get a PhD for this!"

Imagine the weight of that moment: After a decade of dedication, vigilance, and painstaking effort, he could have compromised his integrity for a bribe. The trust of millions— people who had no idea their eyesight depended on his diligence—rested on his choices when no one was watching. What Fienberg preserved wasn't just the nation's sight; it was his own clarity of purpose.

---

[13] AAS Solar Eclipse Task Force, "Lessons Learned from Plans and Preparations for the 2017-2024 Solar Eclipses," Tuesday, June 11, 2024.

3. Fact orientation

Leadership rooted in facts involves two key practices: internal clarity, and constructive communication.

Effective leaders ground their decisions in facts, not in wishes or assumptions. Leaders must critically evaluate the situation from all angles, embracing both positive and negative realities. This requires self-awareness and discipline to confront difficult truths without defensiveness or denial. In other words, it requires a commitment to brutal honesty—but primarily with oneself. By shining a light on the full spectrum of facts, leaders ensure that their decisions are informed by reality rather than wishful thinking. A leader who evades hard truths risks basing decisions on false premises, undermining the community's progress. By acknowledging what's working and what isn't, leaders gain the clarity needed to adapt, solve problems, and set realistic goals. This honesty also helps leaders discern what is achievable for the group and what is beyond reach, allowing them to focus resources effectively.

Once the facts are clear, leaders must distill and share them in a way that empowers the community. This involves presenting information that is relevant, actionable, and balanced. Highlighting challenges while also emphasizing strengths or opportunities creates a framework for collective problem-solving. Leaders should focus on helping the group understand how the facts impact their shared goals and how they can navigate obstacles together.

When sharing difficult facts with the community, a thoughtful approach is essential. While unfiltered honesty can be valuable internally, it may be counterproductive when directed outward. This doesn't mean challenges or setbacks should be hidden; it means they should be communicated with sensitivity to their impact. Effective leaders engage empathy and respect, focusing on solutions rather than negativity. By conveying difficulties calmly and constructively while simultaneously acknowledging their effects on the community and its goals, leaders can maintain trust and morale even in the face of adversity.

"We had our best estimates of how many people we could anticipate," says Rachel Laber Pulvino, Visit Rochester's vice president of communications, who led the region's outreach efforts for the travel bureau. "It was all based on what cities of a similar size in the path saw during the 2017 eclipse, so we were going off our best-educated guesses."

Rochester officials estimated that between 300,000 and 500,000 visitors would travel to the six counties that make up the Greater Rochester area over the long eclipse weekend. This projection was largely based on the experience of Greenville, South Carolina—a city with a similar population (about 210,000, compared to Rochester's 210,000 within city limits and 1 million in the metro area)—which saw roughly 500,000 visitors for the 2017 eclipse. In anticipation, all Western New York schools were closed on Eclipse Monday, and many businesses declared it a holiday. However, while Rochester's hotels were filled to capacity the weekend before the 2024 eclipse, an unfavorable weather forecast for the area south of Lake Ontario led many visitors to shift their plans at the last minute. On the day of the eclipse, thousands of would-be Rochester viewers dispersed two hours southwest and northeast in pursuit of clearer skies, making it nearly impossible to get an accurate count of how many actually remained in the area.

Fact orientation isn't about dwelling on what's wrong or unattainable; it's about balancing the realities of the present with the possibilities of the future. It keeps leaders and communities grounded, helping avoid unrealistic promises that could lead to failure. By focusing on facts and communicating them thoughtfully and constructively, leaders foster trust, clarity, and collaboration, enabling the community to work together effectively toward shared goals.

Thanks to the advance predictions of cloud weather experts, Rochester's task force leaders were aware that their chance of seeing the Sun at 3:20 p.m. on any given April 8 was only 51 percent, so they made it part of their strategy to prepare locals for what to expect from a cloudy-day eclipse: The world would go dark—pitch dark—with an eerie golden glow all around the horizon. By setting appropriate expectations, they were able to minimize the disappointment that residents felt when comparing their experience with those in the path who had clear skies. "The clouds reminded me of that movie," one woman told Rochester's News 10 NBC shortly after totality. "Moses parted the Red Sea and all those clouds. That's what it actually looked like."

4. People orientation

People orientation goes beyond simply enjoying the company of others; it's about truly understanding, valuing, and utilizing the unique strengths, needs, and motivations of individuals to achieve collective goals. In goal-oriented communities, leaders not only build strong connections but also foster an environment where every member feels empowered to contribute in meaningful ways. Effective leaders relish the opportunity to meet new people and deepen existing relationships, uncovering what makes each person unique and what drives them. By visibly taking joy in these connections, they set an example for others, signaling the value of the relationships within the community and setting a rhythm that can be adopted by others. This enjoyment does more than set an example—it actively creates bridges between individuals, knitting together a community that might otherwise remain fragmented.

As Robert Putnam notes in *Bowling Alone*, the erosion of social capital has left many communities struggling to connect across divides of background, perspective, and experience. Leaders step into this gap, performing the hard and necessary work of fostering what Putnam calls "bridging social capital," which connects diverse groups. By understanding and appreciating people on a personal level, leaders create pathways for individuals who may not see eye to eye to find common ground. The leader's role as a bridge-builder is not only about understanding but also about modeling connection, demonstrating that even the most disparate individuals can become part of a cohesive whole.

A people-oriented leader prioritizes relationships, not just roles. They take the time to know who their members are, what drives them, and what unique skills or perspectives they bring to the table. These authentic connections build trust and a sense of belonging, creating a strong foundation for collaboration and commitment to the community's goals.

Cherilynn Morrow is the outreach director for NASA's PUNCH (Polarimeter to Unify the Corona and Heliosphere) Mission, which launched in early 2025 and aims to understand how the Sun's corona becomes the solar wind that affects Earth's atmosphere, causing (among other phenomena) the Northern

Lights. Morrow and her team built an outreach program around the 2023 and 2024 eclipses to help generate awareness of solar science.[14]

"Our PUNCH Outreach team works with many different types of people who may not at first identify with participating in science," says Morrow. "Yet we have learned time and again that if we show up with a bridge-building attitude of respect and openness to mutual learning, we find these same people become our collaborators in creating improved products and methods that benefit everyone." "People *must* feel the respect they deserve," affirms Wales. "Only then can the conversation productively shift to the subject under discussion. Relationship first; content second."[15]

One of the most rewarding—and also the most challenging—aspects of leading a community with diverse skills, backgrounds, and resources is that, unlike in bonded communities, most of its members are unlike one another. When harnessed effectively, this diversity is a bridging community's greatest strength. Bringing together such a richly varied network requires leaders to sharpen their awareness of what makes each individual unique and find ways to inspire them to contribute their strengths to the collective effort. It also requires identifying gaps and seeking the right people to fill them.

---

[14] Cherilynn doesn't just teach science—she *embodies* it. The morning after the 2023 annular eclipse, my wife Gill and I went to meet her beside the "Rock of the Sun" petroglyph, a figure carved into sandstone, in Chaco Canyon, New Mexico. She gave us a thermoform tactile art representation of it that we traced with our fingers, eyes closed. Using the shapes we could feel on the molds, she told us—her voice full of wonder—that it could be a depiction of the Sun's corona during a total solar eclipse in 1097 CE, using the shapes we could feel on the molds to link ancestral skywatchers to modern solar science. It was like standing at the edge of time. *That's* how you do outreach. —*Jamie*

[15] Wales, *The Seven Rules of Trust*, 103.

This approach starts with a fundamental principle: You cannot assume anything about a person—their values, knowledge, or potential contributions—until they show you themselves. This has implications beyond basic cultural sensitivity: It means setting aside preconceptions and creating space for genuine discovery. By engaging openly with each individual, you gain a clearer understanding of what motivates them, what they care about, and how their abilities can best serve the shared mission.

This isn't just an abstract commitment to diversity; it's a strategy for real progress. When people feel truly seen and valued for who they are, they engage more meaningfully. While nurturing such connections takes time and effort, the reward is a stronger, more cohesive community built on trust and shared purpose. By listening carefully, understanding what drives those around you, and connecting people whose strengths complement each other, you foster a culture of mutual support. And when community members feel that their personal goals are valued alongside the collective mission, they invest more deeply, creating an environment where both individual and group success thrive.

5. Emotional stability

Emotional expression is essential for human connection and authenticity. But effective leadership requires considering which feelings to share and tailoring them to the audience. Positive emotions, like joy in the group's purpose or pride in members' achievements, can almost always be expressed unreservedly, as they strengthen community bonds and keep people motivated. But the weight of the inevitable stress, frustration, and disappointment that accompany any leadership effort are the leader's responsibility to manage without transferring their burden to the community they're leading.

Think of it like parenting: You don't want your children managing your stress or fears; instead, you create a stable environment where they feel safe while you handle your emotions appropriately. The same applies to leadership in communities or organizations. "Emotional regulation is an essential part of leadership," says Russo. "Managing your own emotions allows you to contain others and to respond with reason when others are frustrated, critical, or overwhelmed."

Like any external event or challenge, a leader's emotions are facts that need consideration. However, unlike those external factors or even the emotions of others, they are yours alone to regulate; for the health of the community, you can't inflict them on everyone else. Put bluntly: Everyone else's negative emotions matter, but yours don't—except, of course, to you.

So wise leaders cultivate the ability to acknowledge their emotions privately while ensuring they do not destabilize the group. At the same time, though, they must also stay attuned to the emotions of others, and manage these as they do any other facts. The collective emotional state directly shapes a community's cohesion, morale, and overall direction; stress, frustration, and other challenges can ripple through a group, affecting both productivity and engagement. Leaders need to be alert for these emotional undercurrents, addressing concerns as they arise to foster an environment where people feel safe, valued, and heard. Striking this balance between acknowledging emotions and maintaining stability builds trust and resilience, whether in a team, a community, or a family.

This does not, however, mean a leader should suppress his or her own negative emotions; to the contrary, they can serve as important signals that something needs attention, so it is unwise to pretend they don't matter. Rather than internalizing them in isolation, leaders should cultivate a network of trusted confidants outside the immediate community—spouses, friends, mentors, or therapists—who can offer both emotional support and valuable perspective. Engaging these allies regularly helps leaders process challenges constructively while maintaining their role as a steady presence for those they guide.

"My wife, Becca, has been my sounding board from early on," says Dan Schneiderman, whose daughter was born shortly after he became the Rochester Museum & Science Center's eclipse partnership coordinator. "It was difficult balancing having a new kid and diving deep into the world of eclipse organizing. There were late nights, meetings that went long, a summer where I was out almost every weekend, but we always had each other's backs. In the days following the eclipse, Becca was thanked by more people than I can recall for putting up with everything."

Managing everyone else's emotions at the same time as keeping your own carefully calibrated can make leadership a lonely enterprise at times; it can be one of the most difficult aspects of a leadership effort. Expecting this to be the case and preparing your own separate support network early can prevent you from being blindsided and overwhelmed when it happens.

6. Flexibility and strategic agility

While having a clear vision is crucial for guiding a community, leaders must remain flexible in how they define success. The outcomes you envision at the start of an endeavor are rarely identical to what will ultimately be achieved, and clinging too tightly to specific results can hinder growth and innovation. Instead, define your goals as a broad, adaptable framework focused on the overall impact you aim to create rather than rigid, predetermined outcomes. This flexibility allows leaders to adjust as circumstances evolve and new opportunities emerge.

One important goal, in addition to the stated purpose of the group, should always be the cultivation of a healthy, sustainable community that, if possible, endures beyond the initial reason it came together. (Chapters 7 and 8 address strategies for this.) This requires leaders to actively listen to diverse perspectives within the group, recognizing that their own initial ideas may need to shift in response to the experiences and insights of others. By incorporating feedback from those most affected by the community's work, leaders ensure that the goals remain relevant and rooted in the collective needs of the group.

Flexibility also promotes resilience: Being willing to adapt goal-setting as circumstances evolve in response to a changing landscape enables leaders to make meaningful progress toward shared aspirations. Initially, Debbie Ferrell envisioned a small local festival for Geneva, to be held on the north shore of Seneca Lake and sponsored by local business owners. "But it did not end up as that at all," she says. "In the initial stages, I planned and held several community meetings for businesses, nonprofit leaders, city and county staff, the welcome center, library, college and astronomy buffs." Despite city officials' apprehension ("If we have a festival, people are going to come…" and that, in their view, was not necessarily desirable), more community members signed on enthusiastically, the concept evolved, and the list of planned community events for the eclipse grew into the hundreds. "And that was a lot for a small city of 12,000," she says. Eventually, Geneva's "Embrace the Dark" celebration drew about 20,000 people from all over the world.

Strategic agility is the ability to recognize when a plan is failing and pivot decisively toward a better course of action, not just as an internal adjustment but as a collective shift that engages the entire community. It goes beyond flexible thinking—acknowledging the need for change—to actually guiding a group through the process of adaptation, often in the face of uncertainty or resistance.

Strategically agile leaders are attuned to signs that a strategy is faltering, whether through feedback, performance metrics, or shifting circumstances. They don't ignore red flags for fear of sunk costs or personal attachment to the original plan. Instead, they assess the situation honestly and make timely decisions to adapt. This decisiveness helps maintain the community's momentum, minimizing wasted resources and morale loss.

Sometimes, a leader must engineer a pivot all by himself or herself. Eric Michael "Sully" Sullenberger, a middle- and high school physical sciences teacher in Russia (pronounced Roo-shee), Ohio began preparing his community for the 2024 eclipse immediately after experiencing the 2017 eclipse in Perryville, Missouri. At Russia's small rural school, which houses about 450 students from prekindergarten through grade 12 in a single building, Sully dedicated seven years to eclipse preparations. His efforts included engaging students in citizen science, securing grants for equipment, organizing public outreach events, collaborating with local leaders to distribute eclipse glasses, and sparking excitement through teaching, community talks, and hands-on educational activities. His dedication to the effort was unyielding. But just before all of his hard work was about to pay off in early April of 2024, he got sick.

The weekend before the eclipse, I started to run a high fever, just as a couple of the projects I had been struggling with were beginning to come together. My wife is convinced that I wore myself out and that weakened my immune system, causing me to get so sick. I spent all day Saturday in my classroom with a fever, but then wasn't able to get out of bed most of the day on Sunday and kept ticking off one more thing that I wouldn't be able to wrap up as the day went on. When it turned to late evening and I still hadn't made it back to my classroom, I was lying on my back in bed with tears streaming down my face, realizing that I had to let a lot of it go. Being the only person in charge of everything meant that the viewing event was going to have to be nixed. Everyone was very understanding, and I managed to drag myself to school the morning of the eclipse to at least bring some materials home to watch it from there instead. Around noon I went outside, still running a fever, and set things up and prepared to watch.

However, despite dragging the data sensors home from school that morning, I was too worn out to set them up. I was able to see phenomena that I had overlooked in 2017 (especially because it had been cloudy for a bit during the early partial phases). I wasn't able to get much more than a handful of cameras and telescopes aimed at the

Sun, but was able to enjoy the whole eclipse. After the chaos of preparing, it was nice to be able to relax and enjoy it with my family. As soon as totality finished, my phone started blowing up. I was getting phone calls, texts, instant messages, and emails from family, friends, current and former students. Everyone wanted to share their own experiences with me.

Strategic agility is about flexibility without losing sight of your vision, the ability to adapt to changing circumstances while maintaining a clear focus on the overarching mission. When faced with unexpected realities, Sully embraced what his circumstances demanded, and his supporters rallied to make the best of the situation. That spirit of resilience became a core part of the story they will all share for years to come—one they might have preferred to end differently, but will treasure nonetheless.

CHAPTER 3

Drive

There is something unique about the total eclipse
experience and something unique about the people
who chase them: our outlook, our connection, our
gratitude. I really did feel that someone should
explore this further; it took me a little while to
figure out that someone actually should be *me*....
These people are my tribe.

—Dr. Kate Russo, Being in the Shadow,
from *The Path to the Path* documentary,
American Astronomical Society

I came from a very poor background. I was not
able to go to good schools and was always told that
because of that I would never be able to do the
type of science, to do astrophysics like I wanted to.

When I found out that they were wrong—and by the way, all of you, I am *DOCTOR Henry Winter, astrophysicist*—it was a feeling of empowerment. And I want to share that feeling of empowerment with other people who might have been told that they can't do the things that they want to do and to work with them in order to find ways that they can.

—Dr. Henry "Trae" Winter, ARISA Lab, in *The Path to the Path* documentary, American Astronomical Society

The people involved in the AAS task force are great. They're not paid to do what they do; they do it for the love of this thing. Some of them are doing it just for the love of eclipses. Some of them are doing it for the love of spreading science. Some of them are doing it because they know that a little bit of effort can go a long way to spreading the word about what this eclipse is.… Life is about writing your own story and you want this to be part of your story. You want this to be a chapter that you look back on and you talk about for the rest of your life.

—Debra Ross, co-chair, AAS's Solar Eclipse Task Force in *The Path to the Path* documentary, American Astronomical Society[16]

The most important factor in whether a community effort succeeds or fails is not simply who is in charge—it is whether people

---

[16] Ella Ross, *The Path to the Path* The American Astronomical Society Solar Eclipse Task Force. 2023. https://thepathtothepath.org/.

feel excited enough to keep pushing forward. Cultivating that excitement is one of the leader's primary responsibilities; it's why leaders must be cheerleaders at heart. Drive is the engine of leadership.

There are two aspects of motivation: first, a leader must be able to fuel themselves; second, they must be able to transfer that energy to others in a way that sustains momentum over time.

Motivating Yourself

Self-motivation is the foundation of leadership. Without an internal source of energy, even the most capable leaders will burn out before their efforts can make an impact. Key to success in starting an effort and maintaining momentum is to recognize that you must be the source of your own fuel. Pats on your back need to come, first, from your own hands.

Being self-fueled means embracing the reality that no one is going to push you forward except yourself. It means finding ways to keep going even when the work is exhausting, even when progress is slow, even when no one is watching. Leaders must develop a relentless passion for their work, not because they expect recognition, but because they know the effort itself has value. The goal is not to be fueled by applause or external rewards (as welcome as those can be), but by the satisfaction of putting something meaningful into the world. A leader must be their own source of validation, able to look at the community they are shaping and see, in both visible and invisible ways, how their work is creating connections, opening opportunities, and making things possible that otherwise would not have existed.

"I lost count of the hours, the days, the weeks of work I did," says Russo about her effort to promote the eclipse experience in her own community in North Queensland, Australia, in 2012. "Nobody was sharing anything about the wonder and awe of the eclipse; media reports focused on the expected visitor numbers and potential income for the region. So, I went everywhere to share the wonder and awe of totality. I did radio shows, TV interviews, and media briefings. I went to shopping centers, markets, cafes, schools and universities. When anyone asked me to do something, I said yes. Because it was *my* community, and I knew what was to come, and I wanted everyone to experience the awe and wonder of totality for themselves."

Especially when a catalyst like an eclipse has inspired the creation of the community, it is hard to know where, exactly, the work needs to be done, and who needs to be brought into the effort. So a large part of the initial work is in outreach to people who might possibly be interested in joining, or at least knowing about it. Unlike established projects with clear stakeholders, large-scale community efforts often begin in uncharted territory, requiring organizers to identify and engage key players from scratch.

Dan Schneiderman describes one of the biggest challenges in organizing for the 2024 eclipse as not just managing logistics but as figuring out *who* needed to be involved in the first place. He couldn't assume that the right people would simply appear, so he cast the widest possible net, reaching out to a broad and sometimes unexpected range of groups in the hopes of making the right connections. "I chatted with schools, I chatted with senior centers, with universities, with businesses, with chocolatiers, with funeral homes, hospitals, government officials, photographers... you name it, I reached out to them," he says.

He understood that the process would be unpredictable, but he also knew that *not* making the effort to engage widely would mean missing critical partnerships.

This kind of outreach requires persistence and creativity. It means initiating conversations without knowing where they will lead, following up on vague leads, and sometimes persuading people that they *should* care about something they hadn't yet considered relevant to their work. Many of the most valuable partners Schneiderman found were not the obvious ones—collaborations emerged from unexpected places, and often it was the least likely stakeholders who became the most enthusiastic participants. His experience underscored a truth that every community leader must embrace: Before you can organize effectively, you have to do the invisible work of figuring out *who* belongs at the table, and that process takes time, effort, and a willingness to reach beyond the usual circles.

Celebrating yourself is a vital habit to cultivate. When external recognition is rare, it's essential to reflect on your achievements and give yourself the credit you deserve. One effective strategy is to look back and mentally thank your past self for the efforts that led to meaningful outcomes. Reflecting on the positive results of your hard work—whether it's the relationships you've built, the systems you've improved, or the goals you've achieved—can provide a sense of fulfillment and remind you that your efforts matter. This self-reflection does more than boost your morale; it strengthens your motivation to tackle the challenges of leadership, including the tedious or difficult tasks that are often invisible to others. By recognizing and celebrating your own contributions, you sustain the resilience and energy needed to lead effectively, even when the road ahead feels long and uncertain.

There will always be moments when motivation lags, when the weight of leadership feels overwhelming, and when exhaustion makes even the most dedicated organizer question whether they have the energy to keep going. In those moments, the key is not to retreat inward but to look outward—to find others who share similar responsibilities, who are working toward parallel goals, and who can offer both practical support and emotional solidarity.

For many leaders preparing for the total solar eclipses of 2017 and 2024, the American Astronomical Society's (AAS) Solar Eclipse Task Force (SETF) became an essential community. Initially formed as a network of scientists and educators, the SETF expanded over time to include experts from a wide range of disciplines, including tourism, emergency management, and arts and cultural organizations. In the years leading up to the eclipses, the SETF organized in-person and online workshops, sharing best practices for managing large-scale community events, distributing accurate information, and preparing for the unprecedented influx of visitors to eclipse-path communities. These meetings did more than provide logistics and strategy—they connected people across North America who might otherwise have felt isolated in their efforts. Participants not only shared knowledge but also built deep professional and personal relationships, reinforcing the idea that no one had to do this work alone.

"I've been working very, very hard," Trae Winter said during the SETF's final in-person workshop in San Antonio, Texas, in October 2023. Winter is one of the founders of the Advanced Research on Inclusion and STEAM Accessibility (ARISA) Lab, which spearheaded participatory science efforts for both the 2017 and 2024 eclipses. "One of the things about an eclipse is that you can't push that deadline back. But that tiredness has gone away, because now I am with people who, even if I don't know them, they're my friends because we have a similarity of purpose, we have similar passions, and we are not competing. We all want to work together to make things better for everybody. And that's something that you don't always find. And that makes me excited and ready to do the next thing. Maybe after a nap."

"Family support is crucial, but comes at a cost—leaders' loved ones frequently absorb the additional burden of neglected personal commitments," notes Russo. "Recognizing these challenges, it is vital to establish a strong support scaffold for leaders, ensuring they have a network to draw energy and encouragement from, particularly in the final weeks leading up to the event. Holding dedicated check-ins, not to focus on logistics but on the well-being of those in leadership roles, can provide a necessary psychological reset."

The sense of connection and mutual recognition that the SETF fostered was particularly powerful in the final days before the 2024 eclipse, when stress levels were at their highest. Organizers across the country were juggling last-minute logistics, responding to unexpected challenges, and grappling with the immense pressure of knowing that thousands—sometimes hundreds of thousands—of people were relying on their efforts.

With this in mind, the SETF hosted a private online meeting specifically for community leaders just six days before the eclipse—no outsiders, no press, just a place to be their authentic selves. This was not a logistical planning session; it was a space for emotional processing. Many organizers in attendance had reached a point of exhaustion, and this meeting allowed them to step back for a moment and acknowledge what they were feeling. It was an opportunity to see one another, to express the collective stress of the moment, and to be reminded that they were not alone. Russo donned her clinical psychologist hat and facilitated the discussion, helping participants rate and articulate their emotions and recognize the magnitude of what they had accomplished. "Leaders were able to openly discuss feelings of isolation, burden, and lack of balance," she reports. "Verbalizing these struggles and receiving reassurance from peers that these challenges were a normal part of the process was immensely validating."

But looking outward for support is only one way that leaders sustain themselves. Just as important is looking outward with curiosity and learning to be fueled by the invisible good—the positive ripple effects of your leadership that you may never see or hear about. The networks you build, the inspiration you provide, the doors you open for others—many of these contributions will unfold beyond your line of sight, but they are no less real. There is an incredible source of energy to be found in witnessing the ways that others, inspired by the community, take what they have learned and apply it in new and unexpected ways. A leader who recognizes this can, in turn, be fueled by the efforts of those they have supported.

The most effectively self-fueled leaders are those who understand that their work does not end when an event is over, nor does it end at the edges of their own direct influence. The true measure of leadership is not just in what is built, but in what continues to grow beyond the leader's reach. Those who gathered for the 2024 eclipse will carry that experience with them, and some will be motivated to create, to build, to push forward in ways that no organizer could have predicted. Leadership, at its core, is about fostering the conditions for these moments to happen—knowing that the work extends beyond what is visible, and trusting that the impact will continue long after the leader's own involvement has ended. Harrison Nir, one of the producers of *Totality*, a documentary by Sandbox Films, spoke at the September 2023 SETF workshop about the potential long-term effects of eclipse organizing: "What if we saw the eclipse as a starting line, not necessarily for ourselves who are already invested and involved, but for everyone else who we've succeeded in safely ushering under the umbra? With that many geniuses inspired, imagine what we could accomplish."

Community leadership is a constant process of building: building relationships, building structures, building bridges between people and resources. If a leader can recognize that every new success within the community is, in some small way, connected to their efforts, they will find motivation not just in their own accomplishments but in the accomplishments of those around them. To sustain themselves, leaders must develop the ability to celebrate the progress of others as if it were their own. They must look at the networks they have cultivated and understand that the impact of their work extends far beyond what they can directly see. Some of the greatest effects of leadership happen in ways that will never be traced back to the leader, but they happen nonetheless.

Motivating the Community

If self-motivation is the first requirement of leadership, the second is the ability to spread that motivation to others. A leader's energy sets the tone for an entire community. If a leader is passionate, engaged, and enthusiastic, that enthusiasm becomes contagious. If they are disengaged or uncertain, those around them will hesitate to commit. This is why relentless enthusiasm is one of the most powerful tools in leadership. Janet Ivey-Duensing, who worked on 2017 eclipse outreach efforts with communities in Tennessee and South Carolina, saw firsthand how a leader's attitude could shape an entire town's level of investment. "Where leaders were enthusiastic and fully invested, the excitement trickled down, and everyone in their communities embraced the eclipse," she explained. "But where regional leadership was disengaged, a few dedicated individuals had to undertake a herculean effort to drum up even modest interest." A leader does not have to have all the answers or guarantee a specific outcome, but they do have to believe in the work. As Trish Erzfeld from Perryville put it, "You have to believe in this, or no one will, and you will be doomed to failure."

Leadership is not only about direct involvement; it is also about creating conditions that allow others to flourish. Sometimes, that means actively guiding a process, but at other times, it is simply about offering encouragement at the right moment, letting people know that they are seen and that their contributions matter. "I can't fail to mention the support from Debra Ross and the rest of the SETF," says Vincennes' coordinator Sarah Wolfe. "I would not have felt as capable without Deb's unflinching encouragement as a near-stranger from across the country. She was pulling levers and pushing buttons that I know helped propel us to success in this little corner of Indiana."[17]

---

[17] Sarah brought a level of vibrancy and humor to every interaction with the AAS's task force. At our workshop in Albuquerque in 2023, she persuaded several dozen astronomers, educators, and community organizers to sing the refrain of Europe's "The Final Countdown" —loudly even if not tunefully— which she later incorporated into a Vincennes eclipse video promotion. None of us will ever forget it. –Debra

Keeping a community engaged requires more than just an initial burst of excitement; it requires ongoing effort to sustain motivation over time. One of the most effective ways to do this is by relentlessly seeking reasons to celebrate, and shining a spotlight on successes large and small. People need to feel that their contributions matter, that their efforts are adding up to something greater. A leader who recognizes and affirms these milestones, no matter how small, helps build a culture of motivation and persistence.

This was a key strategy for Debbie Ferrell as she led Geneva, New York's eclipse preparations. For over a year, Geneva held monthly meetings to address logistics—safety, traffic, shuttle buses, restrooms, merchandise, and outreach efforts. The task force grew from three members to about twenty, with much of the heavy lifting done by a small core group of organizers. "I spent about thirty hours a week on this for about fourteen months," Ferrell explains, in addition to her work at Geneva's Business Improvement District and running her own gallery, Vines of New York. "And those hours increased as the eclipse approached." Ferrell also collaborated with local nonprofits and the library to distribute glasses and bilingual information to Spanish-speaking neighborhoods, ensuring the event was inclusive and accessible.

Beyond sustaining enthusiasm, a leader's role is also to help people see their own value—not just the importance of the effort itself. The most effective leaders don't just inspire participation; they ensure that individuals recognize how essential their contributions are. People disengage quickly when they don't feel ownership over their own success, and those who are the most capable often overlook their own achievements as they rush to the next task. A leader must take on the responsibility of holding up a mirror, showing people the significance of their role, and making their impact visible—not just to the community, but to themselves.

When individuals believe that their unique contributions matter, they are far more likely to commit fully to the cause. And more than that, when people see themselves as key players in a movement, it changes how they reflect on their own importance—not just during the project, but long after it is over. The leader's job is to ensure that their volunteers, collaborators, and community members don't just feel useful in the moment but look back and recognize their involvement as a meaningful chapter in their own lives.

This process of engagement is not always easy. Not everyone will immediately understand why an initiative is necessary, and some will actively resist involvement. Erzfeld experienced this in Perryville when she struggled to get local emergency management officials to take eclipse planning seriously. "Our 911 director, who should have been on-point in 2017 with the massive planning, was a skeptic, so I got little help from him," she recalled. "If someone is in disaster control, they will be completely uninterested in event planning." Rather than give up, she found a way to communicate the importance of the effort in terms that mattered to them. "I told them, 'You had better know where my event planning ends and your disaster control plan begins.' Only then did they start attending my meetings." Selling a vision often means framing it in different ways for different audiences, helping people see how their involvement directly benefits them and the larger community.

In the end, motivation is the engine of leadership. A leader must fuel themselves first, but their greatest task is ensuring that their energy spreads to others. The ability to sustain enthusiasm, celebrate small wins, and reflect back to people their own potential is what turns a movement from a passing moment into a lasting force. Leadership begins with the question: *If not me, who?* But answering that question requires more than just stepping up—it requires learning how to keep going and how to bring others along for the journey.

CHAPTER 4

Leader Expectations

Sometimes, leadership means taking the wheel yourself—no passengers, no support, just determination to keep going. For Rik Yeames, a sixty-five-year-old Domino's pizza franchise owner from Concord, New Hampshire, that wheel belonged to the "EclipseMobile," his own black Dodge Challenger whose hood he emblazoned with images of a solar eclipse. The vanity plate read, "ECLPS24."

In 2021, Yeames persuaded the New Hampshire Legislature to declare April 8, 2024 as Solar Eclipse Day. It was a rare success with the government in his nine years networking to spread the word about the coming eclipse. "No one wanted to plan ahead," says Yeames, citing the unique challenges of organizing an event centered on totality that was to occur three hours north of Concord in a remote part of the state.

Despite setting up the New Hampshire Solar Eclipse Task Force, tirelessly traveling to give talks, and hosting online events, Yeames found himself largely unsupported. The EclipseMobile wasn't just a vehicle; it became his loudest voice in a mission that often felt like a solo journey.

The journey had a happy ending in New Hampshire. For the day of the 2024 eclipse, Coös County was gifted with spectacular weather that boosted Yeames' outreach efforts, bringing more than 200,000 people to the area and $80 million to its economy. After the eclipse, Yeames placed his vanity plate and memorabilia into a time capsule at Concord's McAuliffe-Shepard Discovery Center, to be opened on the occasion of New Hampshire's next total solar eclipse on May 1, 2079.

The lesson for leaders? It's worth doing even if it turns out the parade you're leading is tiny at first. Encourage everyone to climb on board, push the pedal, and build the bandwagon as you go.

While communities may appear to be just groups of people, not every group qualifies as a community. In contrast with groups that exist because their members are bound by obligation—e.g., children who must attend school, employees who don't like their job but need the paycheck, and people who attend family gatherings out of a sense of duty—true communities are voluntary.

Their members participate by choice, drawn by a shared alignment with the community's goals and values. People join and stay in healthy communities because they see value in spending their most precious resource—time—in ways that enhance both their personal well-being and the collective vision.

Starting with realistic expectations is crucial when leading a community. Without them, you may define success by misguided metrics, leading to dissatisfaction with both the process and outcomes, and a loss of motivation. This can result in overwhelming disappointments or unforeseen challenges that derail your efforts entirely. To prevent these pitfalls, it's vital to approach leadership, especially in volunteer-driven initiatives or professional roles, with clarity and realistic goals. Here are the key principles to guide you.

Expectations for Leaders in Bridging Communities

1. Expect to find only a few like you.
2. Expect recognition for your effort to come later, if at all.
3. Expect varying degrees of success.
4. Expect others' motivations to differ from yours.
5. Expect ebb and flow in participation.
6. Expect friction from within the community.
7. Expect varying levels of honesty.

1. Expect to find only a few like you

Leadership requires extraordinary effort. As discussed in the previous chapter, leading a community effort means committing to long hours and relentless dedication to your cause.

However, to make the journey both sustainable and enjoyable, it's essential to identify others who share your commitment and values—people willing to work hard alongside you and embrace the spirit of giving their all. Finding such individuals will not only lighten your workload but also will infuse energy and camaraderie into your leadership experience.

A small, focused team can be invaluable, particularly in the early stages. If you have the luxury of starting well in advance, focus on achieving small, manageable milestones. These early wins don't have to require massive effort but should be significant enough to build momentum and demonstrate progress. Identifying and celebrating these milestones will energize your team and give your community tangible proof of what's possible, laying the foundation for broader involvement.

Trish Erzfeld, who successfully organized Perry County, Missouri's 2017 and 2024 eclipse experiences, emphasizes the importance of carefully selecting your team. Her advice: Identify and recruit a small group of highly motivated individuals early in the process. Look for people who are not only movers and shakers in your community but also for those who consistently get things done. Erzfeld's guiding principle is clear: "Keep your core group small." By working closely with a handful of capable, self-driven individuals, you create a strong and cohesive foundation for your community effort.

2. Expect recognition for your effort to come later, if at all

Before you begin, acknowledge the uncomfortable truth: Your efforts may go unrecognized, especially early on. External praise will be rare, and your ability to celebrate progress and stay motivated will often come down to your own sense of purpose. It's a leader's job to celebrate rather than expect to be celebrated; this fosters collaboration and strengthens the community. "Leaders don't toot their own horn. They toot other people's horns. That's their job," says Erzfeld.

External validation of a community's efforts might never come, so leaders must sustain the enthusiasm and momentum from within. "You need a leader to rally people and say, 'Let's do something. We need you to be engaged,'" says Rachel Laber Pulvino, a key promoter of Rochester's 2024 eclipse efforts. Erzfeld adds that while collaboration is widely valued, "few may be willing to give up recognition to reach it." True leaders don't seek the spotlight; they shine it on others.

Leaders should also prepare for their expertise to be overlooked. Mark Howell, a veteran in emergency management and planning, was a key figure in Oregon's 2017 eclipse response but found his expertise dismissed when he moved to Missouri before the 2024 eclipse. "Few people really cared or seemed inclined to accept help," he recalls. No one seemed to understand the possibilities in terms of likelihood or magnitude of potential visitation and disruption. "Unfortunately, in my area and many areas nearby, folks were unable to get over long-standing feuds, petty and unrelated disputes, and egos to put together a unified planning front or response effort," says Howell. "My big takeaway from all of it is "focus on the goal" and don't let egos or personal history get in the way. See how folks can contribute to the effort, and then allow them to do so to the best of their ability and desire to help."

For Angela Speck, leadership emerged unexpectedly. Moving from the United Kingdom to Illinois in 1999 and then to Missouri in 2002, she saw the potential of the 2017 eclipse for science outreach and advocated for a task force. Though hesitant to lead, she realized the role aligned with her passion for science literacy. "It had the potential to be good for me personally, but also good beyond me—and those two things put together made it almost inevitable," she says.

Leadership is rarely glamorous. "The leader is not the person taking the limelight but the person who can see the big picture and how all the pieces fit together," Speck explains. She emphasizes the importance of uniting diverse perspectives: "You might have two people in a group who might not understand each other, but as long as the leader understands both, it's OK."

For many leaders, there's a natural hope that their dedication will be met with some form of poetic justice—even if not unmitigated success, at least smooth operations. If your catalyst is an eclipse, what happens in the sky reflects on this emotional investment. "I put my blood, sweat, tears, and soul into this event," says Laber Pulvino. After years of preparation, cloud cover during Rochester's eclipse felt undeserved. "It felt like we earned that last cherry on top. Of course, that's not how life—or the weather—works," she reflects.

While personal glory isn't the goal, recognition sometimes arrives unexpectedly. "Rochester was so invested in the eclipse that accolades came in for community organizers from many sources," says Dan Schneiderman. He recalls recognition from United States Representative Joe Morelle, New York State Senator Samra Brouk, County Executive Adam Bello, and Rochester Mayor Malik Evans, along with awards such as the *Rochester Business Journal's* prestigious "Forty Under 40" award. The cloud cover on the day of the eclipse made such acknowledgments feel all the more significant to those who had worked on the eclipse for so many years.

Ultimately, leadership in community efforts isn't about applause or career advancement. The true reward is the impact on others and the legacy of a united effort.

3. Expect varying degrees of success

Failure is an inevitable part of leading a community effort, especially one as ambitious as organizing for a large-scale event or initiative. When you're coordinating a diverse group of people all pursuing their own interests and motivations, it's impossible to have everything go perfectly. That's why embracing failure as a learning opportunity, and preparing for it mentally and strategically, is essential.

One way to mitigate the sting of failure is to set up small, attainable milestones worth celebrating. These milestones create a sense of progress and keep morale high, even when other efforts falter. This approach mirrors the philosophy of aiming for "some but not all" success: In a diverse group with varied efforts, some initiatives will inevitably succeed, and those victories help sustain momentum.

Perry County, Missouri, stands as a case study in both remarkable success and inevitable missteps. As the crossroads of the 2017 and 2024 eclipse paths, the county achieved national recognition for its efforts. Yet, their ambition came with challenges. Erzfeld notes the inevitability of some failures when juggling so many responsibilities. "Nobody wants to be the boy that cried wolf," she says. "I didn't want to say thousands of people would be coming to our community, and then they don't show up. But to leave my community uninformed and unprepared would have been worse." She recognized that taking bold steps required risking failure. "You can't be afraid to fail."

Reflecting on the 2017 eclipse, Erzfeld identified areas for improvement, such as recruiting more volunteers for Solarfest and collaborating more effectively with the local library to enhance educational programming. "I feel I failed my community there," she admits. Still, these lessons shaped Perry County's improved planning for 2024, demonstrating the value of failure as a foundation for growth.

Failure isn't always a matter of what goes wrong—it can also stem from managing perceptions. Laber Pulvino recalls how cloudy weather the morning of the 2024 eclipse led many visitors from out of town to change their plans, diverting to other locations. Despite Rochester's meticulous preparation, some locals were critical. The Genesee Transportation Council had planned for years to manage the traffic gridlock that typically occurs right after totality ends during a sunny day eclipse, with successful outreach campaigns encouraging locals to stay off the roads unless they were attending eclipse events. But the clouds scattered eclipse chasers to the southeast and northwest, with the result that at 3:20 p.m. on April 8, the roads were free of backups. Success, right? But of course, some locals complained, asking community organizers where all the predicted traffic was. "You're darned if you do, darned if you don't," reflects Laber Pulvino. Effective leadership often requires accepting that not everyone will be satisfied, even when things go right.

Volunteer leaders have a unique advantage: They can shoulder blame more freely than those accountable to stakeholders, like nonprofits, private companies, or public agencies. Erzfeld acknowledges the importance of taking responsibility when things don't go as planned: "If you likely won't suffer financially or professionally from something that goes wrong, it's easier for you to take the blame." This willingness to absorb criticism can protect the morale of the team and foster a culture of trust and resilience.

Ultimately, expecting failure—and embracing its lessons if possible—enables leaders to take bold steps without fear of setbacks. By celebrating small wins, learning from missteps, and taking responsibility, leaders can ensure that failures become stepping stones rather than stumbling blocks. In the context of community building, failure isn't the end; it's an opportunity to adapt, improve, and strengthen the bonds that unite the group.

4. Expect others' motivations to differ from yours

Leadership in a community effort requires recognizing that each participant has his or her own reasons for being involved. While it's unwise for a leader to be driven by a desire for accolades or personal gain, others may in fact be motivated by such aspirations—and that's not only acceptable but can be beneficial. Their independent motivations mean they are driven to contribute for reasons beyond your persuasion. At the same time, some participants may prefer to support the effort quietly in the background, motivated by belief in the cause or a passion for civic participation. Understanding and valuing these motivations is critical to maintaining harmony and encouraging productivity. Celebrating each person's contributions, no matter their reasons for being involved, creates a positive and inclusive environment where everyone feels valued.

There's often a temptation to bring in high-profile individuals or organizations to lend credibility or resources to your efforts. However, leaders must temper their expectations. "Something valuable that I learned during the eclipse planning is that not all people in high positions are leaders," says Erzfeld. "They do their job, and they may do it very well, but they don't necessarily expand beyond their own business boundaries." Titles alone don't guarantee effectiveness or the ability to contribute meaningfully to the collective effort.

Erzfeld recalls an example from Cape Girardeau, Missouri, the largest city in the state's 2024 eclipse path and an ideal location for an eclipse expo. Efforts to involve Southeast Missouri State University initially stalled. "I assumed that local task force members would facilitate introductions," she says. "Ultimately, I had to personally reach out to the college president to schedule a meeting. It was successful, but valuable planning time was lost."

This experience underscores the importance of identifying individuals who can effectively carry conversations and build connections. While big names can provide visibility, grassroots organizers and "doers" often have greater impact, and the most effective contributions can come from individuals without high-ranking titles or lofty ambitions. These grassroots contributors are the backbone of community efforts: They take on tasks, make connections, and drive momentum in ways that are practical and results-oriented. Leaders should actively nurture and empower these individuals, ensuring they have the resources and support needed to succeed.

As a leader, part of your responsibility is recognizing the roles and motivations of everyone involved. By understanding what drives each participant, you can align their goals with the larger mission, creating a collaborative environment where diverse motivations coexist harmoniously.

5. Expect ebb and flow in participation

One of the inherent dynamics of any community is that its membership will change over time. People join with enthusiasm, contribute meaningfully, and eventually move on. This turnover is not a failure on the leader's part; it's simply a natural part of the process.

Members may leave for various reasons, often unrelated to the community itself. Life circumstances change—people lose interest, relocate, shift priorities, or take on new responsibilities. As Speck explains, "There will be disruption. People get sick, work takes them away. There are all sorts of reasons that things ebb and flow." Accepting this reality allows leaders to avoid taking departures personally and remain focused on the community's larger goals. Effective leaders view these changes not as setbacks but as opportunities to adapt and strengthen the group's foundation. Planning for transitions by building a resilient and flexible structure ensures that others can step in to maintain momentum when needed, keeping the community's work on track.

It's also essential to acknowledge the contributions of those who leave. Even brief involvement can leave a lasting impact, helping to advance the community's goals. Leaders should celebrate these contributions, express gratitude, and leave the door open for those individuals to return if their circumstances allow. "We treated every change in leadership or membership as an opportunity to strengthen our task force by recruiting new leaders or other members who we felt would fill in gaps in the group's expertise or experience," says Dr. Rick Fienberg, one of the American Astronomical Society's main eclipse leaders, "and to inject new energy and insight into our efforts."

By anticipating and embracing membership changes, leaders can maintain an inclusive and adaptable community, ensuring progress continues no matter who is involved at any given moment.

6. Expect friction from within the community

As communities progress from concept to action, disagreements are inevitable, reflecting the diverse motivations, perspectives, and priorities of their members. One common area of conflict arises around the community's vision and goals. Some members may push for ambitious, long-term objectives, while others advocate for smaller, incremental achievements. These differences are natural, especially in a group of diverse individuals, but they can cause friction if not managed effectively. Leaders can address this by facilitating open discussions early to align members with a shared vision while remaining flexible enough to incorporate individual contributions. Clear communication about the overarching mission helps ensure that differing perspectives contribute to, rather than derail, the community's progress.

Another frequent source of tension is resource allocation. Limited time, money, and people resources mean that not every project or priority will receive equal attention, leading to potential disagreements over priorities. In communities that include many separate initiatives, competition for limited resources sometimes exacerbates existing challenges. For example, Uvalde County in Texas comprises two distinct communities; the city of Uvalde, where most of the population lives, and the surrounding Hill Country River Region, an unincorporated community with extensive tourist visitation.

"Government resources and infrastructure were in the city, but were very much needed where the premium eclipse locations were along the path centerline, with fewer people resources," says Dr. Kate Russo, who helped organize eclipse planning in the Texas Hill Country River Region. "Had planning started years in advance, the eclipse could have been the opportunity to find long-term solutions to much wider resourcing issues based on geographical locations rather than remaining within county lines. As it was, the strong will for collaborative working allowed for new alliances to be forged and opportunities created, but existing boundaries and systems were a challenge."

Transparency in decision-making can mitigate these conflicts. By involving members in discussions about how resources are distributed and periodically reassessing needs, leaders build trust and reduce feelings of inequity. Similarly, conflicts over roles and responsibilities can emerge, particularly if some members feel overburdened or underutilized. Establishing clear expectations, encouraging shared ownership, and recognizing contributions—whether large or small—can help balance workloads and maintain harmony.

As communities take on new initiatives, differing definitions of success, cultural or value clashes, and varying levels of commitment can lead to friction. Highly enthusiastic members may take on significant responsibilities out of passion or momentum but can grow resentful if they feel left to carry the burden alone. "One significant challenge is managing the natural entropy that affects all leadership efforts," says Russo. "Over time, without deliberate effort, systems and processes tend toward disorder."

Effective leaders address these challenges by normalizing the natural ebb and flow of participation, celebrating progress over perfection, and reframing setbacks as opportunities for growth. By fostering an inclusive environment where all contributions are appreciated and conflicts are handled with empathy, leaders can sustain unity and momentum, ensuring the community continues to thrive despite inevitable disagreements.

7. Expect varying levels of honesty

As a leader, embracing honesty—both with yourself and in your communication with the community—is essential. Strive for high transparency balanced with diplomatic candor to ensure that your message builds trust while fostering collaboration. However, not everyone involved in your effort will share this perspective. It's important to recognize and adapt to the fact that individuals will bring their own interpretations of honesty and objectivity to the table, which may not align with your approach.

Some individuals may view the community through a perpetually optimistic lens, prioritizing public relations and denying bad news. Their aim may be to protect the effort's reputation, but their refusal to acknowledge challenges can undermine the group's ability to address issues head-on. On the other hand, some may position themselves as "realists," focusing solely on the negatives and constantly highlighting flaws in a way that discourages rather than informs. Their insistence on emphasizing problems can sap morale, even when their concerns are valid.

Additionally, some people may struggle with personal biases, making it difficult for them to be entirely truthful with themselves, let alone the group. Whether due to fear, pride, or a desire to avoid conflict, their actions may unintentionally distort the truth, creating obstacles to effective decision-making.

As a leader, an honest assessment of what may or may not happen can help jolt a community into action. For Erzfeld, it was reminding task force members—including police, fire, 911, the sheriff's department and ambulance services—of the thin line between community planning and disaster control that got the group more focused and honest with itself. She told them that they would need to make the call about if and when the eclipse event became a disaster event. "That may have been a turning point for us," says Erzfeld. "That's when we started playing devil's advocate. 'What if downtown gets gridlocked?' or, 'What if we have a sun worshipper streak naked across the courthouse lawn?' Their expertise and training kicked in, and their ideas, solutions, and resources brought value to the task force."

As a leader, your role is to navigate these dynamics with patience and a focus on progress. Accept that not everyone will operate with complete honesty or objectivity, and avoid becoming overly frustrated by these differences. Instead, focus on guiding the group toward shared goals by fostering open communication and creating a culture where diverse perspectives can coexist productively.

Encourage constructive dialogue that allows for both optimism and realism, ensuring that important challenges are addressed without losing sight of the community's vision. By modeling transparency, balancing perspectives, and keeping the group focused on its mission, you can steer the effort forward, even amid varying approaches to honesty and objectivity.

Managing expectations—of yourself, others, and the effort as a whole—lays the groundwork for success. The next chapter explores specific strategies that leaders can employ to foster collaboration, inspire participation, and guide their communities toward meaningful and lasting outcomes.

CHAPTER 5

Community Architecture

Some communities went big for the 2024 eclipse. Others went *really* big. In Rochester, New York, you might have been forgiven for thinking a race of giants had visited town, observed a solar eclipse, and then left town. Scattered throughout the community were enormous pairs of eclipse glasses—one a permanent fixture in the grounds of the Rochester Museum and Science Center (RMSC), the others traveling to schools, parks, and community events.

At six feet long, the 205-pound glasses were not just fun props but fully functional solar viewers. They became a whimsical, larger-than-life symbol of Rochester's ambitious eclipse outreach program, with Dan Schneiderman, the eclipse partnership coordinator at the RMSC, personally chauffeuring them across town. "The joke behind the dimensions is that they were built for my Subaru," he says.

For Schneiderman, the giant glasses were just one plank in a relentless three-year campaign to prepare Rochester for the eclipse. "I was dedicated every day to promoting the eclipse in the Greater Rochester region, making sure everyone was educated, excited, informed, and safe for April 8," he says. His work ethic bordered on heroic. He delivered 107 talks and attended countless meetings with major stakeholders, government officials and politicians, somehow also finding the time to procure and distribute hundreds of thousands of regular-sized eclipse glasses, convincing local schools to close on Eclipse Day— an eighteen-month slog—and helping to organize a three-day festival at the RMSC attended by 10,000 people. "It was an absurd amount of outreach," he says.

"The giant glasses were such a hit," says Schneiderman. "But they were a pain—there's a part of me that would love to toss them off the top of our observation deck."

In any successful community effort, a leader must play three roles at once: glue, cheerleader, and architect. We explored how to be glue in chapter 2 and a cheerleader in chapter 3; now we focus on the leader's role as architect.

Leaders who build bridging social capital don't just set the vision for what the community might accomplish and hope others will follow; they design the framework that makes success possible. In other words, they create the systems, tools, and structures that allow people to collaborate effectively, pursue their own goals, and contribute meaningfully to the shared mission. As explored in chapter 2, servant leadership isn't about control, it's about empowerment. The most effective leaders build environments where people feel supported, motivated, and equipped to succeed. It means not only providing resources but ensuring they are accessible, practical, and relevant.

How to Be the Architect of a Community:

1. Tune your radar to detect catalysts.
2. Start early.
3. Divide the labor.
4. Provide a place to meet and the reasons to do so.
5. Broaden your community through a lens of inclusion.
6. Design effective systems of communication.
7. Build bridges.
8. Engage experts.

1. Tune your radar to detect catalysts

Recognizing catalysts—those unique opportunities that inspire collective action and create lasting communities—requires cultivating a mindset of curiosity and openness. Begin by training yourself to view the world through a lens of possibility. Catalysts often emerge in unexpected places, so continually ask yourself: *What is happening around me that excites or unites people? What moments or issues have the potential to bring people together for a shared purpose?* This mindset ensures you remain attuned to opportunities you might otherwise overlook.

"You don't need to wait," says eclipse community organizing expert Dr. Kate Russo. "Even if you're not in line for some major event, it doesn't mean that you can't do something yourself. Every community has the capacity to pull together and say, 'Hey, we are unique. We are special. This is what we're all about. Let's put this out to the world.'"

Catalysts frequently align with broader societal or cultural shifts, such as advances in technology, environmental challenges, or significant social movements. Paying attention to emerging trends and staying informed can help you anticipate moments with the potential to galvanize action. Additionally, catalysts often transcend boundaries, bringing together diverse groups of people. Look for events or phenomena that have cross-cutting appeal, like celestial events, significant anniversaries, or pressing challenges that resonate across communities. Some types of catalysts are:

- Nature: Expected seasonal fluctuations, like bird or butterfly migrations or an annual meteor shower
- Culture: Upcoming events like an election, or celebration of past accomplishments—e.g., the Bicentennial of the Erie Canal's opening in New York State
- Crisis: Natural, like floods or hurricanes, or man-made, like political upheaval
- Celebration: Sports team achievements, milestones like school graduations

Engaging actively within diverse networks is another powerful way to identify catalysts. Staying connected to local, professional, and online communities increases your exposure to new ideas and opportunities, so attend events, join conversations, and collaborate with people outside your usual circles. Often, a chance remark, article, or discussion will spark an idea or reveal a potential opportunity to create impact. Similarly, reflecting on past catalysts—what made them successful and how leaders recognized their potential—can sharpen your ability to spot patterns and seize similar opportunities in the future.

Sarah Wolfe, who coordinated Vincennes, Indiana's "Dark Side of the Wabash" event for the 2024 eclipse, insists that the opportunities for leveraging the eclipse went beyond simple financial benefits to a community to something more fundamental about humans: "Here we have another unfathomable event, like COVID-19, that is out of our control. We cannot plan the details of the weather that day. We cannot predict the amount of traffic or the potential emergencies.... We do know, however, that we have been given a gift…we can gather our family and friends… and welcome the darkening sky. We get to chase the divine together and know that a part of it grows in all of us, no matter where we are or how we choose to live."

Not all catalysts will announce themselves as transformative, however. Some may appear small or mundane but grow into something significant through persistence and vision. By cultivating patience and awareness, you'll learn to notice the quiet sparks that could ignite larger movements. Equally important is embracing serendipity, those unplanned moments or unexpected encounters that may provide an opportunity to make a difference. Being flexible and ready to act when these moments arise is crucial to leveraging their full potential.

Ultimately, finding catalysts that help spark community creation is about maintaining a balance between attentiveness and readiness. Staying curious, connected, and open to possibility positions yourself to see and act on the sparks that can light the way to transformative community building. The key is to recognize the opportunities gifted by the universe and approach them first with curiosity, then with vision and deliberate effort.

2. Start early

If there's one critical piece of advice from those who organized events for the 2017 and 2024 eclipses, it's this: *Start much earlier than you think you need to.* For any community effort tied to a specific event or deadline, early preparation is essential. Momentum takes time to build, and in the beginning, others may think you're jumping the gun. While many won't join until the event is imminent, starting with a small, committed group well in advance creates a strong foundation for success. Even if others aren't ready, you need to take the lead and begin.

Starting early also provides time to account for the unexpected and to plan for contingencies. "A common hurdle was the tendency for people to wait until the last minute to make plans, coupled with a widespread underestimation of the event's significance," says Janet Ivey-Duensing, who helped communities in Nashville, Tennessee, and Newberry, South Carolina, prepare for the 2017 eclipse. This lack of early planning led to issues for many Texas festivals during the 2024 eclipse, where poor weather created chaos for unprepared events.

While early planning is crucial, it's equally important to understand that most people won't engage until the event feels immediate. Work pressures and daily life often make anything distant seem irrelevant. However, when the local community does begin to show interest, embrace it wholeheartedly. "About twelve to four months out was a growth period," says Trish

Erzfeld, who saw a surge in Missouri locals wanting to host pop-up campsites, viewing areas, and weekend events. She prioritized ensuring that all contributors felt valued, even for activities outside her direct control. "I wanted them to have successful and memorable events because if they were successful, we were successful as a community," Erzfeld explains.

Starting early not only allows you to lay the groundwork for logistics and partnerships but also gives you the flexibility to adapt as interest grows. By fostering early momentum and welcoming late-stage enthusiasm, you can ensure a smoother, more impactful effort for your community.

3. Divide the labor: decentralize and encourage autonomy

A leader's job isn't to do everything; it's to create an environment where others feel empowered to take initiative. Community efforts, especially those driven by volunteers, thrive when people have ownership of their roles and the freedom to act. This requires a decentralized approach, where responsibility is shared rather than dictated from the top.

The first step is identifying those who can take initiative and follow through. Erzfeld emphasizes the value of a strong core team. "About eighteen months out, we picked out the core members of the task force," she explains, including representatives from key sectors. A small, action-oriented team ensured effective collaboration, with monthly meetings reinforcing shared accountability.

Working groups further streamline efforts, allowing people to contribute based on their expertise while making progress on multiple fronts. While not all groups will thrive equally, the overall effort benefits. "If half the working groups are not doing well but the other half are thriving, then we're succeeding overall," says Dr. Angela Speck of the American Astronomical Society's (AAS) Solar Eclipse Task Force (SETF). She emphasizes that leadership isn't about taking the spotlight, but about "seeing how all the pieces fit together."

The Solar Eclipse Activities for Libraries (SEAL) Project, led by science educators Dennis Schatz and Dr. Andrew Fraknoi, illustrates the power of delegation. By providing materials and training, SEAL empowered librarians to create over 49,000 eclipse programs, reaching millions. "The ones that excited me the most were the ones in which educators enabled their students to actually become the experts," Schatz says. In Marysville, Ohio, high schoolers developed presentations for a community eclipse fair, while in East Brunswick, New Jersey, 108 students became solar eclipse ambassadors, expanding outreach.

Fraknoi highlights the strength of leveraging existing networks: "The volunteers in the project were the librarians—who had plenty of things to do besides worry about eclipses—and the science teachers who volunteered to educate their students, their schools, their districts, and their communities." By deputizing trusted community members, SEAL amplified its impact and fostered lasting educational connections.

Volunteer-driven initiatives rely on intrinsic motivation. "You're not going to find a large number of people who are willing to work as hard as I did without getting paid for it," says Dr. Rick Fienberg, the former AAS press officer turned volunteer. His dedication underscores why empowering passionate individuals is essential for long-term success.

Encouraging autonomy also means reinforcing that individual initiatives that only benefit a few members are nevertheless important to the success of the whole community and should be celebrated as such. "Success for us also meant giving people on the task force the freedom to develop their own ideas and determine what success looked like for their individual organizations," says Rachel Laber Pulvino. "Our role was to support them and encourage creativity. For example, the George Eastman Museum[18] hosted an eclipse event called 'Focus, Click, Totality!' which tied into their photography themes. The Genesee Country Village & Museum[19] created a whole weekend event that was fantastic. Meanwhile, three local breweries teamed up to sell eclipse-themed beers, which were wildly successful. Even chocolatiers created eclipse-themed chocolates.[20] These organizations knew what worked for them, and we encouraged them to take part and contribute in ways that made sense for their missions."

By dividing labor, decentralizing leadership, and trusting volunteers, leaders transform a group of individuals into a motivated, collaborative force. This approach fosters inclusivity,

---

[18] The George Eastman Museum is an international museum of film and photography located on the estate of George Eastman, who founded the Eastman Kodak Company in Rochester, New York.

[19] Genesee Country Village & Museum is a 19th-century living history interpretive museum in Mumford, New York. I spent eclipse day at their Solar Spectacle event with all of my visiting family and friends. See photos at TheEclipseEffect.com. Despite Jamie's request, I did not dress up as a Victorian-era blacksmith for the occasion. —*Debra*

[20] Laughing Gull Chocolates, which created custom designs for the eclipse, was featured on ABC News the evening of April 5, 2024, three days before the total solar eclipse. Online orders immediately flooded in from all over the United States. Fortunately, I had stocked up far in advance, so I had plenty for my guests on eclipse day. —*Debra*

prevents burnout, and ensures that the effort remains dynamic, sustainable, and deeply connected to its mission.

4. Provide a place to meet, and actual reasons to do so

Communities form and flourish around purpose. As already discussed, leaders must provide a clear and compelling reason for members to gather—a unifying mission that sparks engagement and keeps momentum alive. But beyond providing a *reason* to meet, it's also key to provide a *space* to meet, whether one regular place or a variety of reliable places. A dedicated meeting space provides the tangible foundation for community building and ensures members feel grounded in the collective effort. Being able to meet in person fosters strong connections, allowing relationships to form and ideas to flow in ways that strengthen the group's cohesion and energy.

At the same time, online platforms like Zoom have revolutionized how communities connect, expanding the possibilities for participation. The COVID-19 pandemic, while highlighting the psychological toll of isolation, also demonstrated how virtual platforms can serve as inclusive meeting grounds for those who cannot gather in person, ensuring that distance and accessibility do not become barriers to participation. This adaptability has become an essential tool for modern community building, enabling groups to reach far beyond their physical boundaries without losing the essence of collaboration.

The Rochester eclipse task force exemplifies the power of combining physical and virtual spaces. Initially meeting in person in 2019, the group transitioned to Zoom during the pandemic in 2020, which accelerated its growth by lowering the barriers to participation. Members could log in without committing extra time to travel, enabling a larger, more diverse group to engage, even if only as passive observers. When in-person meetings resumed in late 2021, the task force adopted a hybrid format to retain the broader audience they had cultivated. "We had to find a balance between virtual and in-person," says Dan Schneiderman. "But the nice thing about virtual is that anyone could join, so we had a wider reach."

This approach helped the group grow to over 750 members, including 175 active participants and hundreds of lurkers who, while less involved, became informed ambassadors for the community's mission. These lurkers, empowered by accessible meetings, played a crucial role in spreading awareness and goodwill, proving that even those on the periphery of engagement can significantly enhance a community's impact.

As indispensable as virtual meeting platforms have become, the pandemic reminded us of the irreplaceable value of gathering in person—the simple joy of a handshake, the warmth of a hug, or the camaraderie of sharing a drink. "Virtual meetings can be enormously productive. But one limitation is that you do not experience someone's passion and drive, hear their comments and thoughts on various topics, and see how they encourage solutions," says Russo. "With in-person events, the passion, excitement, collaboration and goodwill are palpable—and contagious."

Physical connections foster a sense of belonging and trust that virtual interactions, no matter how innovative, cannot fully replicate. Even years later, people reflect on how the enforced separation during the pandemic deepened their appreciation for being in each other's presence, underscoring the essential role of shared physical spaces in building vibrant, resilient communities.

5. Broaden your community

As you're considering how to construct a community that reaches as many people as possible, remember that rich diversity requires not just welcoming people of differing perspectives, social, ethnic, and economic backgrounds; you also need to create a space where people of all abilities feel valued and engaged. As Anita O'Brien of Rochester Accessible Adventures explains: "Disability is simply a part of who we are."

True inclusion isn't just about accessibility, it's about ensuring that every person feels expected and welcomed. Leaders who intentionally design their communities and events with this mindset don't just remove barriers; they go beyond their own assumptions and actively seek input from those with lived experience in navigating the world differently. "That feeling of being accepted is inclusion," says O'Brien. "It's that simple."

A truly inclusive community begins by inviting people with disabilities into the planning process from the outset. This means more than just asking for feedback, it means actively recruiting individuals with disabilities to leadership roles, advisory boards, and planning committees. By incorporating their expertise early, leaders avoid last-minute accessibility oversights that can turn inclusion into an afterthought rather than a priority. "You have time to anticipate needs because they tell you which needs exist," O'Brien points out. This approach benefits not only individuals with disabilities but also the entire community, as accessible design often leads to a smoother, more welcoming experience for everyone.

Beyond structural and logistical considerations, leaders must also ensure that meetings, events, and communication methods are accessible. Depending on the group, this might include providing American Sign Language interpreters or closed captioning for larger meetings—much easier these days with recent technological progress—or ensuring event spaces have adequate ramps and accessible restrooms. Helping the rest of the community see through this lens of inclusion early also empowers them to design upcoming events with these ideas in mind. As O'Brien puts it, "You're going to create additional accessible parking spaces because you're going to expect more than the two spaces that your parking lot currently has." Proactively addressing these needs demonstrates that a community values all of its members, not just those who can navigate traditional environments without difficulty.

Ultimately, inclusion isn't just about compliance—it's about building a richer, more connected community. Leaders who intentionally design their initiatives this way will not only reach a broader audience but will also create spaces where diverse voices, experiences, and talents can thrive. By seeking and genuinely engaging people with disabilities, leaders send a powerful message: *You are not just accommodated here—you are an integral part of this community.*

6. Design effective systems of communication

Clear and consistent communication is the heartbeat of a thriving community, keeping members informed, engaged, and connected to both the mission and each other. Without it, even the most dedicated groups can become disorganized, as people lose track of what's happening and where they fit in. A well-designed system ensures that information flows in both directions—leaders provide updates and guidance, while members feel encouraged to ask questions, share input, and celebrate successes. Seek community members with strong skills in speaking, writing, or managing platforms like social media and email; involving them in shaping the system not only gives them a sense of ownership but also fosters future leadership. Most important, communication needs a structure—ideally one that's documented—so it can be followed, refined, and adapted as needed. Without a clear system in place, communication is often the first thing to break down, and with it, the sense of unity and momentum.

For a community to stay vibrant, members need to hear from leadership frequently and meaningfully. A mix of structured and informal updates ensures engagement. A regular newsletter—whether weekly, biweekly, or monthly, depending on the pace of activity—should provide a broad overview of what's happening, including upcoming events, meeting recaps, major milestones, and ways for members to get involved. Between newsletters, shorter updates via email or social media help maintain momentum by celebrating wins, sharing time-sensitive news, or highlighting new opportunities. Meeting agendas sent in advance keep discussions focused and productive, while post-meeting recaps ensure that those who couldn't attend still feel informed and included.

It's also essential to showcase the work of community members, whether through spotlights on individual contributions or recognition of group accomplishments, reinforcing the idea that every effort matters. Additionally, sharing relevant updates from industry partners, government contacts, or external organizations helps members understand the broader context in which the community operates, strengthening external relationships and credibility.

For communication to be truly effective, a dedicated person or small team should serve as the central hub for information flow, ensuring that updates are gathered, formatted, and distributed in a way that reaches all members and keeps the community engaged. While they don't have to generate all the content themselves, they must be reliable, organized, and proactive in collecting updates from sector leaders and liaisons to prevent important information from slipping through the cracks. Maintaining a calendar of events, deadlines, and key milestones is essential to keeping everyone informed, while also acting as a point of contact for questions, ideas, and contributions to encourage engagement. Additionally, regularly highlighting different voices within the community reinforces that communication is not just top-down but collaborative, fostering a sense of shared participation and inclusivity.

7. Build bridges

Effective leaders recognize that meaningful collaboration doesn't happen by accident; it must be actively fostered. While some relationships may form naturally, leaders must be deliberate in constructing bridging social capital, ensuring that individuals who might not otherwise connect are introduced in ways that lead to productive partnerships. This requires more than simply making introductions; leaders must develop a deep understanding of each community member's strengths, interests, and challenges. By thoughtfully pairing people whose skills and goals complement one another, leaders can create a dynamic network where members achieve more collectively than they ever could alone.

A grant from Science Sandbox, an initiative of The Simons Foundation, enabled Schneiderman to design and manage an eclipse ambassador program for the RMSC. In the year before the eclipse, he trained over fifty community organizations to serve as local educators; the ambassadors received training, equipment, and resources to teach their communities about the eclipse and safe viewing practices. Ambassadors received training in eclipse education, basic astronomy, and eclipse viewing safety, plus telescopes with solar viewing filters, solar viewing glasses, and educational materials for information and activities. Decentralizing this science and safety learning ensured widespread access to eclipse education across the Rochester area, effectively extending the museum's reach into diverse communities. "When we launched the RMSC Community Eclipse Ambassadors program, I never anticipated that the ambassador organizations would collaborate so seamlessly," says Schneiderman. "One standout partnership formed between the South East Area Coalition and FIRST Robotics Team 191, the X-Cats, from Joseph C. Wilson Magnet High School. Together, they engaged high school students in constructing eclipse tents with Mylar film windows, enabling individuals with face sensitivities to safely view the partial eclipse phases. They also co-hosted 'Total Eclipse of the Park,' a free and inclusive eclipse viewing party that prioritized accessibility and community involvement."

To start building bridging social capital within and around a community, leaders should become persistent and observant connectors. They should listen carefully in meetings, casual conversations, and even social media interactions, identifying patterns in what people need and what they can offer. When they notice a potential connection—whether between a business owner and a volunteer, a scientist and a community organizer, or an artist and a tourism board—they should take the extra step of facilitating the introduction in a meaningful way. A well-placed email, a shared meeting, or even an enthusiastic recommendation in a public setting can be the catalyst that launches a lasting collaboration. Leaders who make a habit of this not only strengthen their communities but also build trust and credibility, as members see tangible benefits from their involvement.

Additionally, leaders should create structured opportunities for relationship-building rather than relying solely on organic interactions. This could take the form of networking events, working groups, or even informal gatherings designed to encourage cross-sector collaboration. Establishing environments where people feel comfortable engaging with others outside their usual circles helps break down silos and fosters a culture of openness and shared purpose. The most successful leaders don't just connect individuals once; they follow up, encourage ongoing collaboration, and highlight successful partnerships, reinforcing the idea that relationships are central to the community's progress.

Well ahead of the 2023 total solar eclipse in Western Australia, Carol Redford, founder of Astrotourism WA, mentored a camel owner with a budding interest in astronomy about how to use a telescope; she encouraged him to create a unique tourism offering: stargazing in the remote Australian Outback on camel treks. "With a little encouragement, guidance and support, a basic Outback tour turned into a very popular and bespoke eco-tourism offering," reflects Russo. "The eclipse became the focal point for a longer-term offering, highlighting how powerful a joint eclipse and dark sky strategy can be."

Ultimately, a leader's success isn't measured by how many people they know, but by how well they help others find the connections they need to thrive. By making the construction of bridging social capital a core focus, leaders transform fragmented groups into cohesive, high-functioning communities. When done well, this process doesn't just serve the immediate goals of an initiative, it creates a legacy of collaboration and resilience that outlasts any single project or event.

8. Engage experts

Bringing experts into your community isn't just helpful, it's essential. Whether you're planning a large-scale event, responding to a crisis, or simply striving for long-term growth, experts provide critical insights that can prevent costly mistakes and accelerate success. Their knowledge and experience act as a shortcut, sparing your community from trial and error by offering proven strategies and solutions. From event logistics to disaster management, an expert can provide clarity on key issues—such as how many attendees a venue can safely accommodate, how to handle unexpected traffic surges, or what to do if cell service crashes. Leaders who recognize the value of expertise and proactively engage the right people ensure that their communities are equipped with the best possible information from the start.

Beyond practical guidance, experts also enhance a community's credibility and visibility. Having a recognized authority involved can instantly elevate your group's status, signaling to outsiders—including potential partners, funders, and media—that your efforts are serious and well-informed. Experts lend not just their knowledge, but also their reputation, helping to position your community as a leader in its field. This visibility can open doors to greater opportunities, from funding and sponsorships to collaboration with influential organizations. Leaders who actively seek and integrate expertise position their communities as not just passionate but professional, increasing both external interest and internal confidence.

Experts don't work in isolation—they come with their own networks. A well-connected expert can introduce you to additional resources, strategic partners, and even financial backing that might otherwise be out of reach. This was the case in Cleveland, where Jay Ryan, the creator of EclipseOverCleveland. com, tapped into his connection with David DeFelice, a NASA Glenn Public Relations veteran. DeFelice's deep local connections helped Ryan link up with a growing network of institutions, including science centers, libraries, and even the Cleveland Guardians and the Rock & Roll Hall of Fame, all of whom played a role in spreading awareness and preparing the region for the 2024 eclipse.

For experts to be truly valuable, however, leaders must trust and empower them. "I cannot stress enough that if you are a community planner, please rely on the people in your community in these positions—they are your experts," says Erzfeld. Whether it's law enforcement, emergency responders, or media professionals, these individuals are trained to navigate complex situations and can help prevent potential missteps. For example, Erzfeld was caught off guard when a reporter asked how her small town was preparing for a potential terrorist attack— something she had never considered. "We are a rural farming community—terrorism never crossed my mind," she says.

Having a public relations expert on hand to field difficult questions would have been invaluable. Leaders who surround themselves with knowledgeable professionals not only make better decisions but also build a more resilient and well-prepared community, ready for both opportunities and challenges alike.

9. Celebrate emerging leadership

Great leaders don't just guide their communities, they cultivate new leaders from within. When individuals step up with fresh ideas, initiative, and a drive to contribute, they should be celebrated, not viewed as threats. Encouraging and recognizing emerging leaders strengthens the entire community, transforming it into a self-sustaining organism where responsibility is shared rather than hoarded. The best leadership isn't about holding onto control—it's about distributing it wisely, ensuring that the community thrives long after the original leaders have stepped back.

Fostering new leadership also injects energy and innovation into the group. As new voices gain confidence, they bring fresh perspectives, challenge existing assumptions, and refine strategies for achieving shared goals. Rather than resisting these shifts, strong leaders recognize them as signs of success: a community capable of producing leaders is one that will continue to evolve, adapt, and grow. By mentoring and uplifting emerging leaders—giving them visibility, responsibilities, and opportunities to contribute—established leaders create a culture where participation is both valued and expected.

Ultimately, leadership should never be about gatekeeping; it should be about empowerment. A truly effective leader works toward the day when others are ready to take the reins, ensuring that progress continues beyond their own tenure. When leadership is treated as a shared effort rather than a singular role, the community flourishes—not only in the present but in the long-term legacy it leaves behind.

CHAPTER 6

Get Started

"The world was suddenly fascinated by darkness," says Kirstyn "Kiki" Smith. "I happen to be completely blind, and I found it fascinating that everyone was so excited about darkness for three and a half minutes."

For Smith, outreach and fundraising coordinator at the South East Area Coalition in Rochester, the 2017 eclipse had been a painful reminder of exclusion. As her teenage sons giddily prepared to watch the partial eclipse, she felt sidelined. "I felt very alone," she told the *New York Times*. Diagnosed with a degenerative condition as a child, Smith had lost the last of her vision in 2011. The eclipse, with its intense media coverage and widespread excitement, "was about experiencing a historic moment in community, and I wasn't part of that."

Determined to ensure the 2024 eclipse would be a valuable personal and community experience for everyone in Rochester, regardless of whether they could actually see totality with their eyes, Smith organized an inclusive event, as part of "Total Eclipse at the Park" at Rochester's Genesee Valley Park, for blind and visually impaired individuals. "The largest percentage of legally blind individuals are over the age of 65," says Smith. "They often also have dual disabilities—hearing loss, mobility challenges, memory impairments. We wanted to create a really neat audio, tactile, multisensory experience for those individuals."

The gathering featured a handheld device called LightSound, which translates changes in light intensity into musical tones. As the Sun's light wanes and returns, participants hear the eclipse as a melody, transforming a visual event into an audio experience. Also on offer were tactile maps of the path of totality across the United States and descriptive audio of what was happening in the sky.

Smith wasn't alone in her mission. A team led by Allyson Bieryla, a Harvard University astronomer, designed and distributed around 900 of its LightSound devices across the United States. "My motivation came from thinking about the accessibility of our teaching labs on campus at Harvard and wanting to make sure that we had some resources for students with disabilities," says Bieryla. "What keeps me going is the wonderful feedback and positive response from people that have used the device."

True community-building requires more than just gathering people in the same place, it requires intentional inclusion so no one feels sidelined.

Healthy communities of different sorts of people—bridging communities—don't just form spontaneously as bonding communities do. They are deliberately shaped by fostering inclusion, bridging gaps, and leveraging unique contributions. In this chapter, we explore the blueprint for creating vibrant and resilient bridging communities, using powerful lessons from eclipse task forces, from how they were initially formed to how they evolved over the two catalysts in 2017 and 2024.

1. Leverage your identified catalyst
2. Choose a basic structure
3. Find your people
4. Embrace diversity and inclusion
5. Convince people to join
6. Get political support
7. Attract a mix of personality types
8. Don't rely on bureaucracies
9. Leverage authority and trust

JAMIE CARTER & DEBRA ROSS

1. Leverage your identified catalyst

A catalyst can be the spark that ignites your community, but it does not automatically lead to widespread support. Unlike naturally bonded groups that form around shared interests, bridging communities require a deliberate act of connection. The key to leveraging a catalyst effectively is recognizing that it alone is not enough to unite people—leaders must actively shape the conditions that bring individuals from different backgrounds together. This means identifying what about the catalyst makes it compelling, ensuring that its value is widely communicated, and providing structured opportunities for engagement. The goal is not just to generate excitement but to transform that excitement into sustained participation.

One of the advantages of a catalyst is that it arrives externally, independent of any one leader's vision. This removes the burden of persuasion—leaders are not imposing an idea but responding to an opportunity that already exists. As a result, people don't feel they are merely signing onto someone else's agenda; rather, they see themselves as part of something bigger, something inevitable. A well-leveraged catalyst feels like a gift, not a demand, so the role of the leader is to create a framework that allows people to step forward and claim it as their own. By de-emphasizing the leader's sense of ownership and instead emphasizing shared momentum, leaders make it easier for diverse individuals and organizations to align their efforts under a common cause.

To sustain engagement beyond the initial draw of the catalyst, leaders must create structured ways for people to connect, contribute, and see their role within the larger picture. The most successful efforts don't just harness enthusiasm—they direct it into meaningful action by identifying clear goals, breaking them into achievable steps, and celebrating progress along the way. This turns a temporary spark into a lasting engine of collaboration, ensuring that the catalyst doesn't just generate interest but leaves behind a legacy of strengthened community bonds and continued collective impact.

2. Choose a basic structure

Different community structures bring unique strengths and limitations when responding to opportunities like an eclipse or challenges such as a natural disaster. Their design, resources, and priorities shape how they act and adapt.

Voluntary and grassroots communities thrive on passion, flexibility, and the ability to mobilize quickly. They rely on the creativity of their members and local connections to leverage opportunities that might benefit the wider region. In disasters, they can rapidly assemble volunteers to address immediate needs like food and shelter. However, their informal nature often limits their ability to sustain long-term efforts or coordinate large-scale initiatives.

Formal groups like for-profit businesses and not-for-profit organizations offer structured governance, significant resources, and credibility. Nonprofits might lead campaigns to leverage a perceived opportunity or manage recovery from a disaster, leveraging grants and professional networks. Businesses can sponsor events, deploy supply chains, or fund relief efforts, often aligning their actions with strategic goals. While effective at scaling impact, these entities may lack the agility of informal groups and can face bureaucratic delays or competing priorities.

Bonded and geographic communities, such as religious groups or neighborhood associations, are rooted in shared identity and place. They excel at fostering strong interpersonal connections and providing emotional and practical support. To leverage an opportunity brought by a catalyst such as an eclipse, they might host culturally significant events or promote local tourism. In disasters, their local knowledge and tight-knit relationships enable them to coordinate recovery efforts effectively. However, their focus on internal cohesion may limit broader outreach or adaptability.

Online and hybrid communities combine digital connectivity with elements of other types. Online communities can amplify efforts globally, sharing information or raising disaster relief funds, while hybrid groups integrate grassroots energy with formal structures for coordinated action. These communities are highly adaptable and scalable but may face challenges translating virtual engagement into real-world impact.

There are strategic advantages and disadvantages of each approach, but in practice, a mix of both is ideal, especially for a large scale effort. That's a fine line. "There's an advantage to having authority," says Dr. Angela Speck, who valued the endorsements that the American Astronomical Society's (AAS) Solar Eclipse Task Force (SETF) received from NASA, the National Science Foundation (NSF) and the National Oceanic and Atmospheric Administration (NOAA). "At the same time, being able to be an individual and have the freedom to push a little is helpful," she says. "You have to find ways to be in both places—you want to be both official and not official—and there are ways of doing that."

"Every community faces the dilemma of 'who's in charge.' Unlike other events, no one makes the decision to 'host' a total solar eclipse, so there is no one authority in charge," says Russo, who, for the future Australian eclipses, is starting processes using a bottom-up approach. "Of course, some planning and coordination needs to be managed at the local, county, state, and even national level, where the priority is on resource coordination and risk management. But once communities realize they can create their own strategy, they can just go for it."

In practice, a task force that appears to be packed with experts can sometimes backfire. "We're at a point in the history of the world where often people don't trust experts," says Speck, whose position as a professor of astrophysics is a pigeonhole that's difficult to escape from. "There are some people who think you can never look at the Sun, and you're never going to win over those people no matter what you tell them," says Speck. But there was a solution.

Speck handed over a lot of outreach to students, who tend to encounter less pushback from members of the public with an anti-authoritarian nature. "Students are young and don't yet come with the expert label," says Speck. "They can more easily proselytize to the public—in this case, about safety and where to get the best view of the eclipse."

The lesson is clear: You need the authority to be taken seriously in some places, but you also need to be able to step away from that to be taken seriously in others.

The status of a task force is important, but it's only a foundation—what matters more is who's on the task force and how respected it becomes.

3. Find your people

A community's success will rely heavily on the passion and dedication of its members, regardless of its status. There may already be a naturally bonded community interested in an endeavor. For an eclipse, that's astronomers, who are typically the only group of people who know an eclipse is coming to their community—often decades ahead of time.

Starting with a bonded community is wise—but extending to build a bridging community is essential. "In the very earliest task force meeting that I went to in 2015, it was mostly amateur and professional astronomers, and not very many of the other types that eventually joined us, like transportation folks, emergency management folks, and tourism folks," reports Dr. Rick Fienberg about the AAS SETF. "As we recognized more and more the need to involve these other constituencies, we did more outreach to them, and by 2019, when we restarted the effort for the 2024 eclipse, it was a pretty broad group."

Widening the net beyond astronomers was a priority for its leadership. "You need to be very intentional in who you choose to pull into a task force," says Speck. "It's crucial because there are so many aspects of what needs to happen and so many different things that could be done. We had conversations with people, and then started to build a picture of the people that should be involved."

There were three stages to the evolution of the members of the AAS SETF: astronomers, then astronomers who branched out into specialist and/or niche areas that would be hugely valuable, then community specialists from across the spectrum.

Purposely spreading the net wider is key, but there are obvious bull's-eye people, those whose superpower is also their network. "It was deliberate, but it was organic," says Speck. "My superpower is networking, and that's also how I think of other people." The aim was to bring in people with their own networks to create a never-ending web.

That alone might get you to a bonded community. To go a step further in creating a bridging community requires doing something else—you ask the people you have chosen to recommend others. This is exactly the kind of work that will result in a bridging community.

To take a bonded community beyond its limitations means using a very special skill that instantly elevates an endeavor and yet is so often underestimated as a leadership skill: networking.

Initial recruits for the AAS SETF were astronomers who had unique skills no one else could offer. "It was mostly astronomers that had other aspects," says Speck. "I used my own network, and it spread from there."

An early recruit was Dr. Tyler Nordgren, a professor of astronomy who was not only an eclipse chaser but a space artist who created stargazing-themed poster art for US National Parks. Another was Dr. Pamela Gay, an educator and podcaster at the long-running *Astronomy Cast*. Also joining the group was Michael Zeiler, a cartographer from Santa Fe, New Mexico, skilled at developing cutting-edge and highly instructive and shareable maps and outreach material. The involvement of Russo, a consultant to guide strategic community eclipse planning, a psychologist/researcher who put words to the experience of totality, and who is skilled in media engagement, was a no-brainer.

Convincing people to get involved is a critical step. "In most cases, people were excited to be involved," says Speck. "It had been so long since there had been a total solar eclipse in the

US that there were a lot of people already excited about how it could fit with what they do." For those already involved in science communication, working on the eclipse wasn't extracurricular but an obvious new outlet.

"Then we really branched out," says Speck. Additions included Mario Motta, MD, a cardiologist and a former trustee of the American Medical Association (AMA), and Laurie Radow, who had recently retired after a career with the United States Department of Transportation. Both helped the task force address two issues critical to an eclipse—eye safety and traffic issues—outside the direct experience of the current astronomy-focused members. However, a key addition ahead of the 2024 eclipse, cited by Speck, was Trish Erzfeld from Perryville, MO, who brought to the AAS SETF a powerful new perspective about the eclipse that had already proven successful.

Perryville was one of the few communities positioned in the paths of both the 2017 and 2024 eclipses. That positioned Erzfeld uniquely to assist communities preparing for 2024. Her lack of scientific expertise might have seemed a barrier, but it proved an asset. "I'm a tourism director, not a scientist. My community didn't even understand what an eclipse was," she recalls. Overcoming imposter syndrome, she dove into educating herself and her community, transforming skepticism into enthusiasm. "I wanted people to understand that this was more than just an event, it was an investment in our town's future," she says.

Her emphasis on collaboration and inclusivity became a blueprint for others. Perryville's 2017 task force included over fifty local leaders, and by 2024, she had galvanized an even broader coalition, rallying business owners, civic groups, and residents to create SolarFest. "If you want it to reach its full potential, this cannot be a one-organization event," says Erzfeld. Her success wasn't just in attracting visitors but in leaving a lasting legacy of community pride and cohesion. "When the eclipse is over, your community must be happy because these are the people you will see in the grocery stores, gas stations, and church," she says.

Communities, groups, and organizations only have strength in depth. Creating a successful coalition of people to prepare a community for any purpose therefore requires an effort to identify and attract diverse participants.

4. Embrace diversity and inclusion

Building a bridging community hinges on embracing diversity, not as a buzzword but as an essential foundation for a results-driven network. Diverse individuals contribute unique perspectives, attitudes, knowledge, and networks, strengthening the community's ability to connect and engage widely. Thriving communities draw on these distinct contributions to build broader connections and a shared purpose. "If everybody has the same perspectives and agrees with each other, you might as well do everything on your own," says Speck.

Even among seemingly similar individuals, their varied experiences add value. "Everybody brings something," she emphasizes. "Put that together in a group, and you've got something that's huge." By intentionally including diverse backgrounds and networks, a community gains the ability to see different angles and understand the perceptions of those affected by its decisions, an indispensable ingredient for success.

Seeing things from a perspective different from our own requires a deliberate commitment to inclusion rather than exclusion, as can be tempting because bonding social capital provides people you already know you can trust. This commitment requires seeking out people whose professions, talents, skills, and backgrounds differ from others. "It's not just what you get from diversity, but how you make sure that you include everyone in what you're doing," says Speck. "Diversity is about how everybody is different—their background, networks, and perspectives—and inclusion is how to keep everybody involved."

Anita O'Brien, executive director of Rochester Accessible Adventures, which provides recreational opportunities for individuals with disabilities and their families, emphasizes that both the planning process and the final outcome should be accessible to individuals with diverse functional abilities.[21] O'Brien points out that one in four Americans lives with a disability, making accessibility not just a matter of equity but also a smart business decision that benefits the broader community. She advises planners to collaborate with disability organizations and include individuals with disabilities on planning committees to incorporate a wide range of perspectives. However, the concept of inclusion goes beyond accessibility, encompassing broader considerations that benefit everyone.

Achieving inclusion is somewhat more challenging than diversity because it has two aspects. "To have everybody's contributions included, and to have everyone on a team feel that their contribution is valued, takes finesse," says Speck. A simple example is the need to mitigate the effect on a group of individuals with a loud voice who drown out others during meetings.

---

[21] Anita O'Brien, "Total(ly) Inclusive Eclipse: Planning through the Lens of Inclusion" (plenary paper at the American Astronomical Society Eclipse Planning Workshop, June 10, 2023).

"Being able to include all the voices is how you take advantage of the diversity," says Speck. "Put diversity and inclusion together, and you have something very powerful for the future of whatever you're doing."

There's also a wider aspect to inclusion. The purpose of inclusion within the network you're trying to build, and of the effort as a whole, is to accomplish something for as many people as possible. That's a vital element of why diversity is so important: Appealing to people with diverse backgrounds and networks also helps you get the word out. Adopting this strategy therefore means thinking about all those people in the outside world who are potential members of your audience that can also be included. "Promoting inclusion within the working group and having all of those different perspectives gives you a better chance of being inclusive as you look outwards to your audience," says Speck.

Cody Cly, a Diné (Navajo) astrophysicist and graduate student at the University of Texas at San Antonio, brought a unique cultural and scientific perspective to the AAS SETF. While specializing in laboratory astrophysics and the study of space dust, Cly also served as a cultural ambassador for Native American communities. "Eclipses happen here no matter what age, technology, or who's occupying the land," he says.[22] His efforts focused on raising awareness of Diné eclipse practices and encouraging broader recognition of Native American contributions to astronomy and eclipse education. "Having Cody on board was amazing because he brings a certain perspective that's very different," says Speck.

---

[22] Eclipse Resources: Solar Eclipse Task Force, American Astronomical Society, AAS Task Force Interviews, "Cody Cly: Raising Awareness of Diné Eclipse Practices." 2023.

5. Convince people to join

Deliberately asking particular people to join an effort is key. So is making the opportunity irresistible to them. Speck knew or got to know the people she wanted to join the endeavor, but she didn't ask them to fill specific positions in the task force outside of their comfort zone. "The key was making people feel valued because of who they were," says Speck. "Leadership is about providing opportunities for people to participate, but on their own terms."

The members of Speck's team understood they were involved because of who they were and what they did. This strategy is fundamental to building a bridging network. It's not "I'm the person with the ideas and we're going this way; follow me," but rather a leader seeing who a person is and letting them know that you want them because of who they are. In a way, you sell that person on themselves. "Get someone to figure out where they fit, and they'll do a better job," says Speck. In short, you let everyone know: *That by being you, you are one of us.*

Some members will be hugely supportive but ultimately involved for their own reasons. They'll be self-fueled for their project but ultimately may want their efforts to be highlighted. If they will likely do what they do regardless of the task force, that's a good fit.

6. Get political support

On a practical level, in creating a community that can get things done, it's advantageous to have those in positions of power on your side. Not only will they be able to further the group's aims, but they bring a valuable perspective on what can be achieved and what cannot.

In United States communities, the involvement of the local mayor can be pivotal. Immediately following the 2017 eclipse, Russo traveled along segments of the path of totality into a number of cities and towns, interviewing a broad cross-section of people from local families up to key politicians. "Mayor support really made a difference," says Russo. "While they remained outside of the everyday process, they often spotted the opportunities, identified someone to look into it, and championed the community champions. Those who had an invested mayor often had the most ambitious and successful plans."

In Rochester, officials from the City of Rochester government and the Monroe County government were kept informed of the pace of local planning and had a realistic understanding of how to support the efforts of those central to the planning in science, culture, recreation, the arts, and education.

"Both our local government—Monroe County and the City of Rochester—were highly supportive," says Rachel Laber Pulvino. "They understood the importance of the eclipse and were as engaged as possible, which made our jobs much easier."

"The coordinated collaboration between Monroe County and the City of Rochester enabled a seamless, integrated, comprehensive approach to eclipse planning," says Dana St. Aubin of the Monroe County Public Safety Department's Office of Emergency Management. "Local government leaders established great working relationships, enabling other relationships to form. To this day, those relationships continue to flourish."

This sentiment is echoed by Rochester Mayor Malik Evans. "I am grateful for—and proud of—the collaborative spirit the Rochester community demonstrated; it is our optimum trait that makes this city one of the top places to live, work, and play."

However, the specifics will differ in every scenario. "[For eclipse planning,] circumstances and challenges vary across the path—from city to rural and from regional to remote—but the same leadership principles apply," says Russo. "Most communities in the path tend to be small, with few resources, and even fewer people on the ground. Often one person is doing the bulk of the work, and being endorsed by the mayor makes the role easier. "If you don't have any recognition, it's hard to know if you're going in the right direction."

7. Attract a mix of personality types

All endeavors need a mix of personalities. A key document that helped many communities organize for the US eclipses was Russo's publication "White Paper on Community Eclipse Planning" (second edition), built upon the hindsight lessons of past decade. Her research on community responses to the 2017 total solar eclipse in the US (as well as previous eclipses around the world) identified four community planning profiles that reveal the dynamics within task forces. Although her work focused on future eclipses, these profiles will help any leader understand members of any coalition for any community-driven initiative.

"Evangelical Embracers," explains Russo, are confident individuals or communities that proactively plan, inspire others, and mobilize resources. They are natural leaders motivated by a desire to impact outcomes. "Community Champions" are dedicated individuals deeply connected to their community, often balancing existing roles. They may face burnout without sufficient support. "Watchful Waiters" are hesitant individuals who observe before participating, often influenced by clear frameworks and evidence of progress. "Unsupported Heroes" are passionate individuals who recognize the importance of an initiative but lack resources and support, leading them to give up.

A successful coalition of people or communities is likely to be a blend of these profiles. Russo's research emphasizes the importance of diversity in perspective and experience, noting that "lasting benefits include new working partnerships, increased community focus, and improved communication strategies."[23]

8. Don't rely on bureaucracies

Getting support from national institutions is wise but not pivotal. "We tried to get a better collection of national, official representatives," says Fienberg, citing the National Science Foundation (NSF) and NOAA. "Neither participated that much," says Fienberg. In practice, task force members in the regions did a lot more.

The elephant in the room for the eclipse, of course, is NASA. Anything to do with space or astronomy is *de facto* associated with NASA. That's despite NASA not having much to do with solar eclipses, which are not connected to planetary missions or astrophysics. That did not matter to the general public, who were pumping search terms like "NASA eclipse" into their search engines in enormous numbers in the weeks and months leading up to April 8. Everyone knew that—especially

---

[23] Kate Russo, "Shining a Light on Communities Within the Shadow," in *Celebrating the 2017 Great American Eclipse: Lessons Learned from the Path of Totality*, ed. Sanlyn Buxner, Linda Shore, and Joseph Jensen, ASP Conference Series, Vol. 516 (San Francisco: Astronomical Society of the Pacific, 2019), 221–227.

journalists, who can see page views for news stories skyrocket if NASA is somehow shoe-horned into the headline.

"NASA is the most identifiable name in the space business—when I travel around the world, I see people everywhere wearing NASA t-shirts," says Fienberg. But NASA had its own ideas. "NASA changed its internal eclipse-related structure and organization [after the 2017 eclipse], and the new people were not nearly as involved as the previous people," says Fienberg. "Although we still had plenty of cooperation, it wasn't what we had envisioned."

The lack of dedication shown by nationwide institutional partners was a disappointment, but it also brought a lesson: Don't rely on bureaucracies. "The people who were most agile and did the most for our combined effort were independent people or people who worked in smaller communities, who weren't part of some massive, slow-moving, supertanker of an institution," says Fienberg. It's very hard to have quick responses from people who are part of a very large, hierarchically organized organization. "You can get a lot more out of a member or a representative from a smaller organization, like a local department of transportation or a local task force."

"One volunteer is worth ten pressed men." It's an old adage that can be applied here. If you go to a big institution, such as a government agency or a megacorporation, you come up against rules and hierarchy. You lose control. "You may get assigned somebody you know is happy to have their name on the list of a task force but isn't personally committed to it," says Fienberg. "Whereas if you're focused on individuals, you're getting people who genuinely have motivation and interest and energy and want to do it—whether it means they have to work harder or not." You might get lucky, as the AAS SETF did in the run-up to 2017.

9. Leverage authority and trust

Gaining the support of national institutions for your endeavor might seem daunting or even unnecessary. However, endorsements from trusted brands can provide immense benefits. For Fienberg and the AAS SETF, NASA, the NSF, and NOAA each conducted their own eclipse efforts but linked them directly to the task force's safety website. These links, particularly the ones from NASA, were pivotal because the search term "NASA-approved eclipse glasses" dominated online traffic, even though NASA doesn't approve such glasses. "The willingness to accept the AAS as an authority came about primarily because NASA endorsed us," says Fienberg. "If the AAS had tried to become the authority on solar eclipse safety and hadn't had the endorsement of NASA, the messaging wouldn't have been as effective."

This alignment allowed the task force to amplify its safety messaging and provided validation that the public trusted. "The most important characteristic of this authority is not their authority itself but how well-known they are," says Fienberg, who thinks that NASA's involvement boosted the overall awareness of the eclipse—another key goal of the AAS SETF.

Fienberg's meticulously curated website became the go-to resource, inadvertently being seen as NASA itself by some sellers. "Some people explicitly contacted me about how to get on the NASA list," he recounted. The collaboration between the AAS and NASA showcased the power of leveraging established trust. "It didn't succeed because of NASA's work," Fienberg admitted, "but because NASA was part of it—even if all they did was give us their logo."

This example highlights the critical role trusted partnerships can play not only in amplifying safety and credibility, but also in overall public engagement.

CHAPTER 7

Community Cohesion and Momentum

"Holy cow!" is a typical response from people witnessing a total solar eclipse for the first time, but for the rural community of Genesee County, New York, a cow was also the centerpiece of an innovative and heartwarming promotional campaign. At the heart of this effort was Genny the Cow, a charming mascot who became the county's solar eclipse ambassador. Through creative storytelling, education, and community engagement, Genny united the county's residents and visitors in anticipation of the 2024 eclipse, proving that community cohesion could be just as important as the celestial event itself.

To engage younger audiences, the Genesee County Chamber of Commerce published *Genny Sees the Eclipse*, a delightful children's book written by Colleen Onuffer and illustrated by Andy Reddout.[24] The story follows Genny and her farmyard friends as they experience the eclipse together, teaching the importance of eye safety and the wonder of this once-in-a-lifetime event. Proceeds from the book were donated to local animal shelters, tying education and goodwill into the campaign's mission.

Genny's influence didn't stop at the page. A life-size cutout of the mascot attended local festivals and events throughout the year, donning her ISO-certified solar eclipse viewing glasses and posing for photos. She also featured prominently on commemorative merchandise including t-shirts, posters, and solar eclipse glasses, reinforcing the campaign's branding: GeneSEE the Eclipse.

The strategy worked brilliantly. Genny became a symbol of pride and connection for the community, inspiring widespread participation and excitement. The campaign not only celebrated Genesee County's agricultural heritage but also turned the eclipse into a shared experience that transcended geography and demographics.

---

[24] More information about "Genny Sees the Eclipse" can be found at TheEclipseEffect.com

By embracing a mascot with local roots and universal charm, Genesee County demonstrated how creativity and community spirit could transform an astronomical event into a moment of lasting unity.

A shared identity allows people from different social groups to bridge their differences, become bonded and collaborate more confidently. However, a shared identity doesn't just happen, it's a deliberate act. From unique, quirky moments like Genny the Cow, creative leaders can quickly encourage the "us-ness" that sets the tone for collaboration.

This chapter emphasizes the strategies that cement cohesion and propel momentum. The key is creating a self-sustaining identity, transforming temporary networks into lasting communities that resonate beyond the catalyst event.

How Leaders Can Encourage Community Cohesion and Momentum

1. Connect everyone, welcome everyone.
2. Sell the community on itself.
3. Craft identity through art.
4. Make meetings memorable.
5. Celebrate success and track progress.

1. Connect everyone, welcome everyone

Connecting people within a community who might not otherwise have interacted is the work of community leadership. It's essential for the people being connected to trust the leader not to waste their time, of course, but if given the permission and latitude to connect, community-driven collaboration becomes a possibility. However, it's crucial to understand that this is not a natural, organic thing in the community, it's the hard work of the leader, who therefore should think actively about every single member of the community and purposely create bridges between them. The same applies to welcoming new faces into an endeavor. Always remain open to diverse perspectives and talents.

As they prepared during the months and years in advance of the 2024 eclipse, each meeting of the Rochester Eclipse Task Force concluded with the leaders asking, "Who is missing from this conversation? Who else needs to be in the room?" Dan Schneiderman says this question originated from a 2016 meeting, at which he represented New York State at the Nation of Makers nonprofit kickoff at the White House.

"Tom Kalil, former deputy director of tech and innovation for the White House Office of Science and Technology Policy, heavily brought up this topic during the meeting," he says, "and it has stuck with me ever since.... I knew that the stakeholder meetings were not a true representation of the region, but often found that attendees had connections from friends and families. From constantly bringing the question up, I ended up having conversations with multiple churches, funeral homes, retirement communities, musicians, and even the DMV."

Continually invite and welcome new voices—not necessarily to become full members of the task force, but to attend meetings. Publicly introduce them and thank them for their contributions, instantly creating an atmosphere of belonging.

2. Sell the community on itself

Building trust is at the heart of any successful community effort. Without it, people hesitate to invest their time, energy, or resources. At its core, trust allows individuals to feel secure in their participation and confident in the vision they're working toward. But trust isn't commanded, it's cultivated. And cultivating trust requires leaders to embrace the art of selling.

Not selling in the commercial sense, with gimmicks or pressure, but selling as a process of persuasion—of communicating a vision so compelling, so grounded in transparency and facts, that people naturally want to be part of it. Selling isn't about coercion; it's about creating an understanding of what the needs are, and persuading people they can fill them.

The best leaders understand this intuitively. They don't issue mandates; they invite people into a shared purpose. Effective communication builds trust by making people feel valued and essential to the effort's success. Trish Erzfeld, who became chair of the eclipse task force for the state of Missouri's 2024 efforts after having had such a successful effort in her region in 2017, says it best: "Make them feel like this event relies on their participation because it really does. Make them feel valued, and they will give you one hundred and ten percent, which will reflect on your community."

Whether rallying volunteers, securing support from local businesses, or gaining buy-in from hesitant officials, Erzfeld's point holds: People commit when they feel seen, needed, and respected. That's leadership through persuasion.

Many people shy away from the idea of being a "salesperson." They associate sales with manipulation or self-interest. But in reality, selling done right is about understanding others, finding common ground, and presenting ideas in a way that resonates.

The first step in persuasion isn't talking; it's listening. Great salespeople and great leaders alike start by understanding the people they hope to engage. What are their priorities? What concerns do they have? What excites them? When leaders take the time to listen, they're not just gathering information; they're demonstrating respect. And respect builds trust.

Next, leaders must frame their vision in terms of shared benefits. People don't engage simply because they're told to; they engage when they see how participation enhances their own lives and strengthens their community. Instead of saying, "We need volunteers," it's far more effective to say, "This is an opportunity to showcase our town, boost local businesses, and create an unforgettable experience for families." When people understand the "why" behind an effort, they are far more likely to commit.

Momentum is another key ingredient. If you ask too much, too soon, people hesitate. But if you create easy entry points— small, achievable steps—they gain confidence and investment grows naturally. A local business owner might not commit to sponsoring an event immediately, but they may be willing to display a poster or donate a small item. Each small "yes" builds toward larger commitments.

Above all, persuasion depends on authenticity and transparency. Trust evaporates when people sense hidden agendas. Leaders who acknowledge challenges, invite honest feedback, and communicate openly will find that even skeptics are more willing to engage. No one expects perfection, but they do expect honesty. And when people feel they are part of the process—not just being dictated to—they take ownership of the outcome.

Finally, participation must feel personal. As Erzfeld points out, people give their best when they know their contributions truly matter. Publicly recognizing even small efforts, thanking people sincerely, and making individuals feel indispensable strengthens commitment and inspires others to step up. Leadership isn't about issuing orders, it's about making people feel like they are part of something meaningful.

At its core, leadership is about persuasion, not authority. The best leaders don't demand action; they inspire it. When leaders embrace the mindset of selling—not in the transactional sense, but in the sense of creating belief—they transform passive observers into passionate participants.

3. Craft identity through art

In any large-scale community effort, crafting a shared identity must be built on vision and trust. But vision and trust alone aren't enough; identity has to be both anchored and communicated. Art serves as a powerful tool in this process, adding a visual and emotional dimension that transforms an event from something that happens into something that belongs to the community.

Rochester's decision to commission Dr. Tyler Nordgren to design iconic eclipse poster art for the city—and then host a traveling exhibit featuring thirty of his creations—was more than a promotional strategy. It was a declaration of identity. The posters depicted local and national landmarks bathed in the glow of the eclipse, seamlessly connecting the event to the region's character while linking the region to the larger, global experience. This artistic representation helped reinforce the idea that Rochester wasn't just witnessing the eclipse, it was an essential part of it.

At an AAS Solar Eclipse Task Force (SETF) meeting six months before the eclipse, SETF leadership distributed to each attendee a signed print of the 2024 AAS eclipse poster Nordgren had created as a lasting symbol of their role in shaping the event. The meeting also featured a display of eclipse-themed merchandise—stickers, mugs, and baseball caps—each bearing slogans, artwork, and most important, the name of the city or community. These items weren't just souvenirs; they were identity markers, allowing people to take pride in their connection to the eclipse and their role in its success.[25]

Art and merchandise are more than tools for visibility; they are mechanisms for fostering identity and pride. They anchor collective memory, giving people tangible ways to connect to the shared experience and ensuring that the event's impact lasts far beyond its fleeting moments. By investing in creative expressions, communities don't just promote an event; they inspire emotional connections that strengthen civic pride, deepen engagement, and leave a lasting imprint on both residents and visitors alike.

4. Make meetings memorable

Boring, pointless meetings are the easiest way to lose members of a voluntary community. But great meetings that help participants feel their precious time has been well spent can be the

---

[25] For the last AAS SETF workshop in September 2023, we asked participants from all over the country to bring us samples from the merchandise their communities had created for the 2024 eclipse; it took four long tables to display all of the t-shirts, mugs, posters, books, stickers, blankets, bags, umbrellas, hats, wine, beer, and, of course, eclipse glasses. At the party that evening, we drew participants' names one by one and gave it all away as door prizes. We had so much that it took almost an hour. People like winning stuff. —*Debra*

difference between a community that lasts and one that falls apart. By blending purpose, recognition, interaction, and a bit of playfulness, leaders don't just run meetings—they can build a culture of enthusiasm, collaboration, and momentum. When meetings are engaging and meaningful, people leave inspired to take action, ensuring the community's work thrives long after the meeting ends.

Open with energy and purpose. The Rochester Eclipse Task Force kicked off each meeting with Schneiderman announcing how many days remained until the eclipse—a small ritual that built anticipation and reminded everyone why they were there. Starting with something playful—a countdown, a 30-second music clip (Vincennes, Indiana opened meetings with "The Final Countdown"), even a quick eclipse trivia question—can create a sense of occasion and make people smile. Keep early updates tight: brief reports from team leads to reconnect the dots from the last meeting and set the path for the current one. If you're using slides, keep text minimal and visuals engaging—humor helps, especially when it's tailored to your group's shared experience. Meetings aren't presentations; they're participation engines. The more you invite energy and rhythm at the top, the more momentum you'll build for the work ahead.

Keep leader updates relevant and engaging. Sector leaders should keep reports concise, highlighting key achievements, current needs, and how their work ties into the larger mission. Long-winded updates lose momentum, so a two-minute time limit per report helps maintain energy. If possible, leaders should bring a prop, visual, or anecdote to make their update memorable. A rotating "mystery update" or surprise announcement can add an element of fun and keep attendees engaged.

Celebrate wins and community contributions. When people feel valued, they stay engaged, and using meetings to recognize both big and small accomplishments keeps people motivated. Leaders should make an effort to collect updates in advance. Lighthearted traditions that celebrate individual contributions (e.g., "paper plate awards") offer a fun way to recognize effort and celebrate personal or professional wins that connect to the mission.

Make guest speakers and expert segments interactive. Long lectures can drain energy, so expert speakers should be encouraged to interact with the audience through Q&A sessions, panel discussions, or live demos. An "Ask Me Anything" format lets members drive the conversation, while pre-submitted questions help surface the most relevant topics. Whenever possible, hands-on activities or small breakout discussions keep participation high.

Encourage cross-sector collaboration. Some attendees may serve as liaisons to industries, governments, or outreach initiatives, so meetings should facilitate networking and collaboration. Leaders can set aside time for introductions, highlight successful partnerships, or encourage a quick "Connector Moment," where attendees identify who they need to meet before they leave. An "Ask & Offer" system where members list one thing they need help with and one resource they can provide can create valuable connections that extend beyond the meeting itself.

Incorporate fun and surprises. Small, unexpected moments of fun keep meetings enjoyable. A raffle with donated items, a surprise guest, or a quick challenge—like a contest for the best themed accessory—adds energy without derailing the purpose. If there's a way to tie a meeting theme into snacks, even better!

Whether it's Moon Pies for an eclipse event or a signature non-alcoholic drink, little details can make gatherings feel more festive. [26]

Close with energy and purpose. How a meeting ends is just as important as how it begins. A quick summary of action items ensures everyone knows what comes next, and a final group moment—like a one-word reflection on the meeting—keeps energy high. A teaser for the next meeting, such as an exciting guest or a big announcement, helps build anticipation and encourages attendance. And always ask the audience who else needs to be invited to the room.

5. Celebrate success and track progress

Just as acknowledging hardship builds resilience, amplifying successes fosters confidence. Every milestone, no matter how small, fuels motivation and reinforces a sense of accomplishment. Community-driven efforts thrive when people see that their work is making a difference. Leaders must make a habit of celebrating progress not as an afterthought but as an integral part of keeping momentum alive.

People who work hard rarely pause to recognize their own achievements, let alone announce them. In a community effort, one person's success is everyone's success—but it's up to the leader to make that clear. Publicly recognizing achievements

---

[26] In Rochester, three breweries—Strangebird Brewing, Three Heads Brewing, and Rohrbach Brewing—teamed up to craft three beers for the 2024 eclipse: Strangebird created "The Lighter Side," Three Heads created "The Darker Side," and Rohrbach created "Totality." Six weeks before the eclipse, we taste-tested these beers at a task force meeting. "The Darker Side" won, but only by a short head; they were all delicious. So we knew to stock up before April; by Eclipse Weekend, they had all sold out. —*Debra*

strengthens the group's sense of shared purpose, deepens commitment, and reminds participants why their contributions matter. Whether it's a successful outreach event, the formation of a new partnership, or a short presentation featuring photos, quotes, or key metrics, celebrating these wins reinforces the impact of the work being done. Success doesn't have to mean a major breakthrough; even incremental progress deserves recognition.

Tracking progress is just as critical as celebrating it. Without a way to measure success, it's difficult to sustain motivation and adapt to challenges along the way. While an entire chapter later in this book is dedicated to measuring impact, one essential principle is worth emphasizing now: Success must be evaluated across multiple dimensions. Too often, communities default to narrow definitions—measuring only financial returns or attendance numbers—when real success is far more complex. How has engagement grown? What lasting relationships have been built? What changes in perception or enthusiasm have emerged? These qualitative victories are just as important as the quantitative ones.

By embedding both celebration and evaluation into the rhythm of community leadership, efforts remain focused, energized, and adaptive. Success isn't a single moment; it's a series of steps, each one worth acknowledging. The more people see the value of their work reflected back to them, the more they will invest in carrying it forward.

CHAPTER 8

Risk, Uncertainty, and Resistance

You're standing beside the Alamo in San Antonio, Texas—the state's most historic site—as the skies darken, the temperature drops, and the Sun's corona blazes into view. For many, this might have seemed the perfect place to witness the 2024 total solar eclipse. Unfortunately, science got in the way, and the historic Spanish mission and fortress became the unlikely site of a modern-day struggle over facts and misinformation.

While much of San Antonio lay within the eclipse's path of totality, its downtown, including the Alamo, did not, and would only experience a 99.94 percent partial eclipse—shy of the awe-inspiring totality. It would be a tantalizing yet ultimately frustrating sight. Despite this, the Alamo's website initially claimed it was "the best place to watch the upcoming solar eclipse." For Dr. Angela Speck, chair of the Department of Physics and Astronomy at the University of Texas, San Antonio and co-chair of the American Astronomical Society (AAS) Solar Eclipse Task Force (SETF), it was a roll-your-eyes moment. "Only the northern and western parts of San Antonio are in the path of totality, so whether you're a San Antonian or a tourist, do not stay downtown, or you will miss the show," she told *Forbes*.[27]

So she deliberately picked a fight with the Alamo.

"It was the right thing to do for my community to make the eclipse as successful as possible for as many people as possible," says Speck, whose cocky demeanor helped her front up to challenges, including being intimidated. "I think about personal risk when planning, and I probably take more risks than most, but I'm not sure I would necessarily tell people to follow my lead." It took time, but the Alamo historic site association eventually changed its messaging. The San Antonio Zoo then unhelpfully announced it would stage an "Eclipse Extravaganza," despite also being outside of the path of totality, having only

---

[27] Jamie Carter, "Forget the Alamo: Why Eclipse Chasers Must Avoid Central San Antonio on April 8," *Forbes*, March 18, 2024.

122

a 99.97 percent partial eclipse. The amusement park Six Flags Fiesta Texas, which was in the path of totality, then revealed plans to launch fireworks during totality. It, too, was also a focus of Speck's ire.

It was all to no avail—the ill-positioned events went ahead, and the pyrotechnics went off at Six Flags. Although Speck wasn't successful with her efforts, she didn't regret taking on the challenge. "They all did their own thing, but I don't care about those organizations," she says. "What I care about is that because of our efforts on social media and local radio, at least some people who might have gone to those places for the eclipse didn't, and they got to have the experience they should have had."

It wasn't Speck who failed—it was those three entities in San Antonio, two of them guilty of ignoring the science, and Six Flags of failing to understand totality. Speck's experience is a reminder that risk and uncertainty are inherent to leadership, but even partial victories can have lasting ripple effects.

Taking on the unknown—creating a new community, designing systems, or striking new ground—can feel like blasting into space without a spacesuit. Traditional views on risk often come from the extremes: Risk assessors highlight every potential pitfall, making failure seem inevitable, while the "just leap" advocates downplay the challenges, pushing bold action without nuance or facing facts. Both perspectives are helpful, but neither offers a playbook.

Even if it has no event planning dimension, community leadership can use an approach to risk that is realistic yet encouraging. This perspective reframes risk assessment as an empowering process of identifying your skills and strengths, defining clear and attainable goals, and recognizing that success isn't all-or-nothing. Combine this with an indomitable work ethic, and risk can be transformed from a barrier into a manageable and even motivating factor.

Risk can become a catalyst for innovation, uncertainty a prompt for adaptability, and reaction to resistance a chance to carve out a group identity—and provide valuable lessons that can guide future endeavors.

1. Understanding risk in leadership
2. Navigating uncertainty
3. Overcoming resistance

1. Understanding risk in leadership

Risk is everywhere, and it comes in many guises. For an event, it could be extreme weather, technology failures, medical emergencies, or even rioting. Being brutally honest about what the risks are, and what the uncertainty is, is crucial if you are to have a plan to mitigate them: Shore up your defenses in advance. "There's always some kind of risk," says Dr. Rick Fienberg at the American Astronomical Society's (AAS) Solar Eclipse Task Force (SETF). "Despite the most careful planning, things won't go the way you expect." It's important that a leader is realistic about the fact that nobody knows what will happen.

The risk-reward equation delicately balances the potential gains of community efforts and the risks involved in pursuing them. It's the art of weighing what could go wrong—be it financial strain, public criticism or burnout—against what could go gloriously right, such as transformative change in a community. For community leaders, dealing with risk is a daily reality.

Risk should be deliberate, not reckless. By identifying what could go wrong, planning ways to mitigate those risks, and moving forward with clarity and purpose, risk can be made into a strategic advantage.

Taking on a leadership role in a high-profile community effort, such as organizing around an eclipse, inevitably comes with personal risks. Reputation is often on the line—leaders can face criticism or blame if the initiative falls short of expectations or if unforeseen complications arise. The emotional toll is equally significant: Leaders frequently pour immense time and energy into their roles, risking burnout or neglecting other responsibilities. Conflicts among stakeholders with differing priorities can strain relationships, and when resources are scarce, leaders may feel pressured to personally invest financially to keep the effort afloat. These challenges highlight that leadership isn't just about managing a project, it's about navigating the personal sacrifices and risks involved.

Some leaders, like Speck, can take bold risks because of specific advantages. "It would be very hard for me to lose my job over something like that," she says, referencing her own tenure and resulting professional security, and her willingness to wrestle with public institutions in the name of science learning. "I can stand up for what I believe in—and there are very few situations where I won't." Leaders with job security can absorb the brunt of blame without jeopardizing their livelihoods, allowing others to focus on their contributions without undue pressure.

Not all risks come from external pressures. Resistance within the community itself can be just as challenging. Trish Erzfeld, who organized eclipse efforts on both local and state levels, encountered organizational leaders who hesitated to commit. "There were other organization leaders in my community that were hesitant to help," says Erzfeld, who had two general responses locally to her appeals for help with staging events, both of which are common in communities:

- The event may be a bust and they don't want to risk potential embarrassment by being associated with it.
- The event was not their idea, so they are unwilling to use their resources and volunteers to support it.

"They always spoke positively about the event, supporting it verbally and encouraging me, but never helped to make the event a success," says Erzfeld. "They just sat back and watched." The experience left her with the belief that leaders need to be very confident and believe in what they are doing if they are to stand any chance in convincing others to risk their reputations. "I knew this event could make or break me professionally, but I had to be the most confident person in the room," she says. "If you don't believe it, no one else will—and I was able to be confident by being honest with my team."

While some in a community will willingly fight for the success of an endeavor, others will actively do the opposite, perhaps because they think resources are being misdirected or simply because of deep-rooted fractures or conflicting priorities.

Artist Sarah Wolfe, whose town, Vincennes, Indiana, hired her as its eclipse coordinator, had to deal with clashing perspectives on the event as part of her community planning. Vincennes' main eclipse event, "Dark Side of the Wabash," featured a "metaphysical alley" where vendors offered crystals and tarot card readings, among other experiences. While most residents enthusiastically climbed on Wolfe's bandwagon during eclipse preparations, other community segments were wary. "I was accused of witchcraft and hosting demon portals," says Wolfe. "There was also a pocket of Evangelicals convinced the eclipse was a sign of the End Times."

The controversy weighed on organizers in the months leading up to the eclipse. Fearing that the intensity of the backlash could derail efforts to create a unifying town-wide experience, they quietly dropped all references to the metaphysical alley from publicity materials. "The issue was that we were seen to be actively soliciting those types of vendors deemed to be questionable in the eyes of some in the religious community," says Wolfe. "So we didn't turn anybody away—that includes churches and religious organizations."

The irony? Wolfe is married to a former Catholic priest who now works as a hospital chaplain. "Sadly, no portals opened," she adds wryly. The eclipse came and went—no cosmic disruptions, just a town standing awestruck after the breathtaking spectacle in their sky.

Leaders often become scapegoats, blamed for factors beyond their control, like weather, traffic congestion, logistical hiccups or even misinformation spread by third parties. Public perceptions often focus on results rather than the nuances of effort and planning, leaving leaders vulnerable to criticism for elements they cannot influence. Even if something is obviously not the fault of anyone, such as bad weather, public dissatisfaction and points of contention can feel like blame.

The only way to avoid this risk is through proactive communication, setting realistic expectations early, and emphasizing uncertainties and the inherent uncontrollability of certain factors, such as weather. For example, eclipse chasers who watch from cruise ships—a common way to reach remote destinations—will typically be given frequent weather updates. This transparent, fact-based approach can help leaders maintain credibility, manage public perceptions, and mitigate unfair criticism later if clouds roll in.

Effective communication about risk is critical. Leaders must provide clear, accurate, and balanced information that allows individuals to make informed decisions. However, leaders should not downplay risks or sugarcoat realities but instead should equip people with the facts they need to evaluate risks and rewards for themselves.

The biggest risk factors for the recent North American eclipses were weather and eye safety. With doom merchants predicting clouds and others assuming the skies would be clear, it was critical for leaders in all communities to explain the probabilities clearly, drawing on historical meteorological data. Similarly, when discussing safety risks, like eye protection during the eclipse, the AAS offered straightforward guidance in simple language about the importance of using certified–safe solar eclipse glasses.

It's critical to formulate the facts to minimize misinterpretation. For the eclipse, that meant people needed to understand the difference between seeing a partial solar eclipse and a total solar eclipse. Only during the latter are there a few minutes in the middle—totality—when solar eclipse glasses might be safely removed, so precise language really matters. "If you tell people that you need to use a filter at all times, except during totality, then there's a good chance that they'll follow the instructions correctly," says Fienberg. "But if you say during totality you don't have to use protection, they might think that they're seeing a total solar eclipse, so don't need protection—and that's risky."

Simplicity, accessibility, and inclusiveness in communication are crucial. To reach as many people as possible, use multiple channels, such as public meetings, emails, and social media updates. Visual aids like infographics or videos can simplify complex information and make it easier to digest. Transparent, proactive communication doesn't just help people navigate risks; it strengthens their connection to the event and the community, turning potential uncertainties into moments of trust and shared purpose.

2. Navigating uncertainty

Uncertainty is a defining characteristic of any large-scale endeavor, especially one as complex and precise as preparing for an eclipse.

Despite the ability of mathematicians to map eclipse paths centuries in advance, the edges of those paths remain imprecise. This uncertainty is not a flaw but a symptom of the fact that scientists cannot measure the Sun's diameter precisely. That means the width of the Moon's shadow is an estimate. In short, all eclipse maps are, to some extent, wrong. This only matters for communities right at the edge of the path of totality, introducing uncertainty as to where exactly is in and out of the path of totality.

In reality, it's rarely if ever an issue, but just a few weeks before the eclipse on April 8, 2024, a new, more accurate map of the path of totality was published.[28] This had real-world implications, especially for places like Montreal's Cité Jardin, which shifted from being within the path of totality on maps used by planners for years, to being just outside it on the new version. The revelation[29] underscored a crucial lesson for leaders: Unexpected developments will reshape plans. It happens constantly in politics, business, and every corner of human society.

"The best-laid plans can go awry, so you need to adapt," says Rachel Laber Pulvino of Visit Rochester. Originally, Rochester organizers planned a Friday night welcome event for media and eclipse VIPs, featuring the Rochester Red Wings playing as the "Moon Rocs."[30] But as bad weather loomed two days before, backup plans were considered. Ultimately, they decided to cancel the event entirely. "There weren't many media in town yet…and it just didn't seem necessary," Pulvino explained. "That decision was a good reminder to remain nimble and always focus on what success looks like." By prioritizing meaningful contributions to the weekend, Visit Rochester could pivot without losing momentum.

3. Overcoming resistance

Resistance is an inevitable challenge in community leadership, often stemming from factors within a community that can't

[28] John Irwin, "Path of the 2024 April 8th Total Solar Eclipse," BesselianElements.com

[29] Although this story fell into my lap, I was always going to write it. The temptation of writing the headline "Why Your Total Solar Eclipse Map Is Now Wrong" was too much. Still, I felt guilty publishing the story, knowing how many of the eclipse event organizers I had interviewed would gulp when they read it. It was one of the most-read articles on Forbes in April 2024. —Jamie

[30] Rochester Red Wings, "Rochester Red Wings to Debut Special 'Moon Rocs' Identity for Solar Eclipse Celebration," March 5, 2024.

easily be appreciated in advance. They include, but are not limited to:

- Skepticism, which arises when stakeholders doubt the feasibility or value of an initiative, particularly if they have been disappointed by failed efforts in the past
- Inertia, which emerges when individuals or organizations resist changing long-standing habits or priorities, preferring the comfort of the status quo
- Interpersonal conflicts, which develop as differing goals, perspectives, or personalities clash, creating barriers to collaboration and progress

"There are certain life events for which we should bury the hatchets, put aside petty squabbles and differences, and get to work," says Mark Howell, about the lack of effective planning in one small community on the centerline of the path of totality. "This was one of those times, and when confronted with 'lead, follow, or get out of the way,' most folks chose 'none of the above.'" He recalls four attempts by three different individuals to form an "eclipse committee" in the local area over the two-year period leading up to the 2024 eclipse in Missouri. Only the fourth attempt gained any traction, with a mere three months to spare before totality.

In Vincennes, there was a lot of malaise and disinterest when the topic of the eclipse was brought up in public forums in the months preceding the event. "I'll never forget the time a woman told me that she 'didn't care for natural phenomena,'" says Wolfe. It was one of many small, rural communities where people panicked about potential overcrowding and trash issues based on misinformation about how many visitors were expected, indicating a need to overcome skepticism with proper messaging.

Although many schools planned years in advance to shut, permit excused absences, or close early on the day of the eclipse—or instead incorporate the celestial event into the day's curriculum as a teachable moment —many did not.[31, 32]

"One of the big struggles I had in planning to lead an event at my school was that my administration didn't think the eclipse would be a big deal," says Eric Michael "Sully" Sullenberger, the physical sciences teacher from Russia, Ohio. "My superintendent had experienced a partial eclipse during an annular eclipse in the mid-90s in Ohio. Partial eclipses can be somewhat underwhelming, especially when you have the chance to see other partial eclipses and they're all kind of the same. So getting him on board took time, which also froze up funding, and also limited the opportunity to fundraise and time that we had to plan. Some of the ideas we had fell through."

For the 2023-2024 school year, Russia's was the only public school district in the area planning to be open on eclipse day. "My superintendent was surprised at how some area schools planned two years early to be closed on eclipse day. We [the 5-6 science teacher and I] were barely able to convince him to buy some eclipse glasses a year early. He didn't think everyone would want to see it and so only purchased enough for the middle and high school students."

So Sully, knowing how important this moment would be to his students, focused on the students' science learning

[31] "Why Schools Are Closing for the Total Solar Eclipse," *ABC News*, April 5, 2024.
[32] Natalie Neysa Alund, "Why Some Schools Are Closing—and Others Are Teaching—During the Solar Eclipse," *USA Today*, April 2, 2024.

132

and preparation, with the help of two $5,000 external grants he secured.

"As equipment came in, my students started to familiarize themselves with it," he says. "By the new year, my freshman classes and solitary physics students were in total eclipse-prep mode. My students researched various citizen science projects that could be participated in, presented them to one another, and trained in doing them. They also helped plan and lead activities for the elementary students, and assisted me with engaging the public in doing citizen science."

It's common for ignorant school administrators to ban pupils from watching solar eclipses, typically on the grounds of health and safety. "In 1979, when an eclipse went over Winnipeg, the school board announced they would pull the curtains and have kids stay inside and watch it on TV," says Jay Anderson, an eclipse chaser and meteorologist who provides eclipse community organizers and chasers worldwide with climate advice for advance planning. About 35 percent of students didn't show up for school that day in 1979—the biggest absentee rate in their history—because parents made the decision to take their kids out of school so they could watch the eclipse.

Even when sound scientific safety advice is offered by experts, the end result can be unexpected. Mark Percy, planetarium director of the Williamsville Central School District in Buffalo, New York, founded the Buffalo Eclipse Consortium and trained community members as "solar eclipse deputies," experts in safely observing the eclipse. "Not only could I achieve my true mission of preparing our community, but it was also a way to cement the planetarium's role as the place to turn to for astronomy information," says Percy. "I was invited to talk to emergency planners, school leaders, town board meetings, and interviewed by numerous local media outlets."

However, his sessions were canceled, and the website was scrubbed of information. "School leaders met without including me and made decisions without my advice," says Percy, who suspects there were liability concerns. He was still allowed to talk to the press, but his responses had to be vetted. He wasn't allowed to respond to emails without express permission. "I know that the school district has dealt with countless sensitive and messy situations," he says. "But this wasn't one of them."

Percy's experience underscores a larger challenge in community planning: the tension between expertise and institutional caution. Whether it's an eclipse, a public health initiative, or an infrastructure project, communities thrive when decisions are informed by those with deep knowledge of the subject. Yet all too often, organizations default to risk aversion—shutting down dialogue, overcorrecting for liability, and excluding the very experts who could help navigate uncertainty.

Public engagement is at its best when leaders trust the public with accurate information rather than restricting access to it. The 1979 eclipse in Winnipeg and the Buffalo eclipse planning efforts reveal a crucial lesson: When institutions fail to lead, communities find their own way. The question for future planning—whether for an eclipse, a natural disaster, or any major civic event—is whether authorities will step up to guide the process or leave citizens to work around them.

CHAPTER 9

Hype, Media, and Outreach

Dr. Tyler Nordgren, a space artist and astronomer based in Ithaca, New York, faced a unique challenge: to create a poster[33] representing the path of totality across New York State during the April 8, 2024 total solar eclipse. This was not merely an art project, it was an outreach tool to inspire and educate the public while also representing the state's diverse regions.

As the creator of iconic, vintage-style travel posters, Nordgren is known for combining scientific

---

[33] TheEclipseEffect.com has this poster and many other examples of Tyler Nordgren's work.

accuracy with visual appeal. For New York State's tourism bureau, I Love New York, his task required prioritizing the facts of the eclipse while showcasing the beauty of the regions within the path of totality.

New York City, 250 miles southeast of the path of totality, loomed large in the state's identity. "I made it very clear that I did not want New York City on there—nor any other big city that was outside totality," says Nordgren.

As he worked to balance scientific rigor with inclusivity, additional complications arose. "I had thought it would just be a nice, simple design, but I had to find a way to include Buffalo, Rochester, Syracuse, the Finger Lakes, and Niagara Falls," says Nordgren. Even after the design was complete, there were objections. "Once it was out on public display, I got a call from some angry tourism folks telling me that I had only included three or four of the Finger Lakes, and there are ten in total," he recalls. By then, it was too late to make changes.

Despite the bureaucratic challenges, the poster became a powerful outreach tool. "When there was disagreement about wording, I let the art drive the message," says Nordgren. The finished poster celebrated Western New York's diversity while upholding the scientific integrity of eclipse outreach.

When organizing a large-scale community event, media and outreach efforts play a pivotal role in shaping public perception, engaging participants, and ensuring the initiative's success. This chapter explores how to effectively harness hype, manage media, and craft outreach strategies that resonate while avoiding pitfalls.

Large-scale community events demand well-orchestrated media and outreach strategies to shape public perception, engage participants, and ensure long-term success. Thoughtfully-designed outreach can foster community identity, control narratives, and create a legacy that outlasts the event itself. From leveraging local resources to managing the pitfalls of overhype and misinformation, the lessons from the 2024 eclipse offer invaluable insights into what works—and what doesn't.

Outreach is the act of sharing information with individuals or communities, but at its core, it's telling the world what you're doing and why it matters. Crafting compelling narratives and leveraging personal stories are crucial for engaging the public effectively.

However, successful outreach efforts involve much more than media strategies that garner headlines; they can keep a community together, moving, informed, inspired, and connected. Outreach can provide the glue and the fuel for the entire endeavor to succeed.

1. Harnessing hype
2. Crafting narratives
3. Controlling narratives
4. Strategic media planning
5. Building trust
6. Building bridges

7. Inclusive outreach
8. Art and merchandise

1. Harnessing hype

"Tens of thousands of people having their minds blown during the most unnatural natural phenomenon you can ever experience."

When you talk about an event in such terms—as Nordgren and many other eclipse chasers did—you enter the arena of hype. Both legacy media and social media run on hype. It's become a necessary method in the face of shrinking attention spans.

The art of hype is made more difficult when your audience doesn't trust the source or has no way of verifying something with their own experience. "It's hard to get people excited about something when they don't know what they'd be missing," says Polly White, whose GreatAmericanEclipse.com website contained phrases like "Solar eclipses are the most beautiful sight you can see in nature," and "It will absolutely blow your mind." "We can use the most extraordinary language, but it doesn't always have an impact," she says.

The driving idea behind the website was simple: high-quality content draws people in. "If you have content that attracts an audience, then you can have things like a store selling merchandise—that's the formula," says eclipse cartographer Michael Zeiler, who is married to White. In advance of 2024's eclipse, GreatAmericanEclipse.com saw four times the business it did for the 2017 eclipse. Leaders can learn from this balance, leveraging excitement to draw people in, and ensuring they stay by meeting their expectations with substance and clarity.

There's a big difference between hype and overhype; the latter can have a detrimental effect on any endeavor. "If anything, there was too much advance publicity in the month leading up to eclipse day," says Cleveland's Jay Ryan, who fears the hype wore out the public before the eclipse happened. "Expectations were raised so high that the actual view of totality did not live up to the hype," he says. Effective leaders frame excitement with realism, ensuring public enthusiasm translates into lasting satisfaction—not disappointment.

2. Crafting narratives

The key is to leverage what people find appealing, focusing on meaningful content that resonates with audiences. The media is constantly seeking surprising angles and new hooks that might appeal to their readers, but what hooks people about an event may surprise leaders.

During the 2017 eclipse, astrophysicist Dr. Angela Speck discovered that animal behavior, almost more than the prospect of seeing the Sun's corona, captivated audiences. So she spoke about it at a NASA press conference on the eclipse, despite her personal ambivalence about it. "I was asked more questions than anyone else on the panel," she recalls, embracing the unexpected interest to engage broader audiences.

Speck's advice? "Throw as much information as you can out" and let the audience's curiosity guide the narrative. "Be comfortable with letting your audience take you where they want to go."

Leadership is not about imposing a rigid vision, but about collaborative storytelling. By meeting people where their curiosity lies, leaders can deepen engagement and broaden the impact of their message. This flexibility transforms a one-way narrative into a dialogue, which encourages trust.

3. Controlling narratives

In Rochester, fact-based outreach was a cornerstone of the city's eclipse efforts. "Much of our work involved managing expectations and clarifying misconceptions," says Rachel Laber Pulvino. Visit Rochester went to lengths to explain that it was expecting 300,000 to 500,000 visitors across the entire nine-county region rather than just to downtown Rochester. Its projections were based on economic and tourism data from cities of similar size in Tennessee that had experienced the 2017 eclipse. "Our goal was to be as open and transparent as possible about our sources and calculations, helping everyone understand the basis of our projections," says Laber Pulvino.

Controlling the narrative means balancing excitement with realism. Savvy leaders manage expectations by framing uncertainties, like weather and attendance, as part of the unique experience. Heather Lerner, an associate professor of biology and museum studies at Earlham College in Richmond, Indiana, witnessed her community's missteps in planning for a flood of visitors that never materialized. She advises focusing on meaningful community engagement rather than speculative numbers. "We missed an opportunity to invite our alums to come back to the college to celebrate with us," says Lerner. "On the other hand, the number of people who came was exactly the number we could serve well. It was incredible."

Both examples underscore the importance of narrative stewardship in leadership. By balancing enthusiasm with realism, leaders can create experiences that inspire and satisfy without overpromising.

4. Strategic media planning

In Rochester, proactive outreach to the media was an important part of its PR efforts. "To garner publicity, I needed the task force members and partners to share what they had planned so I could disseminate that information," says Laber Pulvino. To position Rochester as the ultimate eclipse viewing destination, she needed to know what was happening, and why it was special. "There was a lot of back-and-forth communication with our partners to figure out what was happening and strategies to target the right media so we could tell our story," she explains.

A proactive media strategy involves disseminating press releases, crafting guest articles, coordinating interviews, and equipping stakeholders with tools like templates and pitches to sustain momentum.

"Visit Rochester had two main pillars of PR activity," says Laber Pulvino. "The first was the one most people think of—working with the media, bringing them here, and getting coverage." However, as well as looking outward, Visit Rochester wanted to address the city's residents. "The second, equally important, was local awareness and engagement, ensuring we managed expectations and got everyone on the same page," she says. Visit Rochester worked to bring those two extremes closer together, helping everyone meet in the middle.

Intentional messaging helped Rochester balance enthusiasm with realism, keeping the public informed and avoiding misunderstandings.

Rochester's identity-building efforts were central to its media strategy. As the easternmost major city in the eclipse's path, it faced stiff competition from nearby cities like Buffalo, Cleveland, and Indianapolis. "This was an eclipse of cities, but we did a great job positioning ourselves and promoting ourselves," says Laber Pulvino. By leveraging its unique position and focusing on strategic promotion, the city deliberately distinguished itself in a crowded field.

5. Building trust

Dealing with sensationalism in media further tested the importance of messaging. Headlines about chaos and exaggerated fears about counterfeit eclipse glasses highlighted the media's tendency to sensationalize. In such contexts, Jimmy Wales, founder of Wikipedia, advises "radical transparency."[34] "Transparency is good for trust, and trust is good for people."[35] Proactive leaders like Dr. Rick Fienberg of the American Astronomical Society's (AAS) Solar Eclipse Task Force (SETF) anticipated these issues, recalling that before the previous eclipse, Amazon had issued refunds to customers who purchased solar eclipse glasses that may not have complied with industry standards. So even as media outlets sought and published hype in their never-ending quest for clicks, Fienberg issued timely, calm, fact-based press

---

[34] Jimmy Wales, *The Seven Rules of Trust: A Blueprint for Building Things That Last,* Crown Currency, 2025, 152.
[35] *The Seven Rules of Trust,* 153.

releases about certified eclipse glasses, preventing misinformation from spiraling out of control. [36, 37]

Then, when a sudden surge of fake eclipse glasses actually emerged in the weeks before the 2024 eclipse, Fienberg swiftly pivoted, releasing updated guidance to the press and getting ahead of any potentially misleading articles.[38] His meticulous approach ensured the public received accurate, actionable advice, avoiding a media frenzy. This illustrates how proactive messaging can counter clickbait and protect community trust.

By anticipating challenges and crafting clear, intentional communication, leaders can leave a lasting impression of credibility and reliability.

6. Building bridges

Outreach varied by community, and in some places was limited only by the creativity of those leading the effort. Artist Sarah Wolfe, whose city hired her to help their region plan for the 2024 eclipse, says the city "had no idea what that meant, exactly, and I was given pretty free rein to dream up ways to impact our community," she says.

She gave many presentations, large and small, to community groups, churches, social clubs, and every school in the county. She also met with county and city officials, emergency

---

[36] Chaim Gartenberg, "Amazon Issuing Refunds for Potentially Unsafe Solar Eclipse Glasses," *The Verge*, August 12, 2017.

[37] American Astronomical Society, "American Astronomical Society Offers Warnings and Reassurances About Eclipse Glasses," press release, March 11, 2024.

[38] American Astronomical Society, "American Astronomical Society Warns of Counterfeit and Fake Eclipse Glasses," press release, March 22, 2024.

management planners, street departments, local electrical companies, and school superintendents.

"I ran an occasionally unhinged social media campaign to educate and motivate folks to take advantage of the eclipse opportunities," says Wolfe, who also wrote newspaper articles and newsletters, made TV and radio appearances, ran ads, chucked Moon Pies in parades, and wrangled a musical project to involve the arts across the county. Her humorous videos[39] to teach about eclipse safety reached far outside Vincennes.

The very act of such prolific outreach is community building; it tells the people around you that you have something special to tell and have chosen them. Wolfe's creative efforts united people around the eclipse and established a legacy of enthusiasm for future endeavors. "I still have strangers tell me how awesome it was, their eyes shining with the memory of totality," says Wolfe. "And that feels good."

These efforts not only united her community but exemplified bridging diverse social groups, ultimately leveraging the catalyst to strengthen communal ties.

7. Inclusive outreach

All locations have multiple identities; in any large metropolitan area, outreach must be targeted at various sections of the community. The Dallas–Fort Worth area, which has a total population of 8 million, has 1.7 million Spanish speakers. As eclipse outreach coordinators reached out to the Hispanic community, they found themselves countering some unexpected cultural beliefs; one common misconception was that pregnant women who are in the presence of the eclipse could have a baby with

---

[39] Wolfe's videos can be seen at @vincennesknoxcountryeclipse on Instagram.

facial deformities or birthmarks. A *USA Today* article[40] traces this to an Aztec belief that a lunar eclipse resulted from a bite being taken out of the Moon.

Instead of dismissing traditional cultural beliefs, it is far better to acknowledge their existence and importance within the community and address them respectfully. The Perot Museum of Nature and Science in Dallas developed an inclusive approach to outreach for the 2024 eclipse, sending outreach vehicles and "tech trucks" to disseminate fact-based advice—and 1 million pairs of eclipse glasses—to over 600 schools across the metropolitan area; they also sponsored dozens of astronomers, who staged viewing events at libraries, schools and community centers.

By integrating diverse cultural perspectives into a shared event, inclusive outreach widens networks, creates new collaborations and builds trust. This aligns with the principles of bridging capital by integrating marginalized communities into the shared experience of the eclipse.

8. Art and merchandise

For the 2024 eclipse, T-shirts, posters, mugs, and stickers were not only in demand as consumer goods but were used by savvy communities to spread messages and foster a sense of identity.

For some artists, it was an opportunity like no other. Nordgren wanted to paint the path of totality in its entirety, eventually managing to create forty-six posters in total, from

---

[40] Ashley May, "Pregnant During the Eclipse? Superstitions Say It Could Harm the Baby," *USA Today*, August 18, 2017.

national parks and landmarks to specific locations and events.[41] Given that his art is, in effect, an outreach tool for communities looking to position themselves for the eclipse, the various ways his work was commissioned—and wasn't—is eye-opening, as is how it was used for merchandise.

Many communities were sold on the idea of Nordgren's art, but some built their entire outreach strategy around it. "Brockport was one of those cities in New York that pursued me to design a poster for them," he says. For Brockport, in Greater Rochester, the project was a collaboration between the university and the city—a real "town and gown" effort. They worked together and shared their vision for the design, and the final poster was something everyone adored. The SUNY Brockport Tower Fine Arts Center Gallery even hosted *The Art of the Eclipse: Works by Tyler Nordgren* exhibition—created and toured by the Rochester Eclipse Task Force—in February 2024. However, Brockport then did something unusual: It gave Nordgren's art away.

"What set Brockport apart was their approach to merchandise," says Nordgren. "They gave local businesses permission to sell products featuring my poster design, and I started getting

---

[41] I first met Tyler at the AAS task force workshop in 2019 and immediately recognized the potential of his art to be a unifying force for Rochester's eclipse efforts. He finished the first one for us in early 2020; overall, he created nine regional posters for Western New York; these became the backbone of a 32-poster traveling exhibit selected from his pieces created for the 2017 and 2024 eclipses. Starting in April 2023, we used the exhibit as an outreach strategy by displaying the canvases at a different Rochester location each month for the year in advance of the eclipse. (You can see these at TheEclipseEffect. com.) Just as Dan's Forester seemed custom-constructed for giant eclipse glasses, my Outback was perfectly-proportioned for hauling bulky exhibit boxes between libraries, art galleries, community centers, and restaurants. Yes, we are a people fiercely devoted to art, science, and Subarus. –*Debra*

orders from all kinds of places—bookshops, furniture stores, chocolate shops, you name it."

Brockport's approach exemplifies how leaders can effectively foster both bonding and bridging social capital. By involving local businesses, the university, and the broader community, they created a shared sense of ownership and pride in the event. This collaboration extended the reach of the eclipse beyond a single day and reflected a key principle of transformational leadership, creating opportunities for everyone to participate in and benefit from a shared vision.

Most communities in the path of totality had assumed eclipse-related merchandise would sell only on the day of the eclipse. Brockport had a much shrewder strategy; its businesses bought and sold their stock months in advance. "It must have sold like crazy because they kept re-ordering until a week before the eclipse," says Nordgren. This strategic foresight ensured financial benefits for local businesses and reinforced community identity well before the eclipse.

Most communities—even those that did commission Nordgren—did not have the foresight to use his art to its fullest extent. "Brockport's strategy stood out as a smart, pro-active approach, in contrast to places like Niagara Falls, who waited to put out merchandise until the day of the eclipse," says Nordgren. It's a great example of how leaders should focus on early, deliberate planning to maximize both short- and long-term benefits for their communities.

To use the eclipse to raise funds is something only those with foresight were able to do in 2024. "We made a compelling logo and catchphrase and sold a ton of merch to help cover costs," says Wolfe, whose "Dark Side of the Wabash"—a reference to the lower Wabash River that runs through Vincennes—was cleverly crafted not to attract visitors, but to appeal to locals.

Done properly, outreach is more than promotion; it is a catalyst for creating lasting connections. By balancing hype with realism, crafting inclusive narratives, and using tools like art and merchandise to foster identity, leaders can transform a fleeting event into a lasting legacy. The stories from Rochester, Vincennes, and Dallas illustrate how thoughtful outreach builds trust, bridges diverse communities, and creates shared memories that endure.

CHAPTER 10

Failure and Recovery

I know all about spending years planning for and then missing totality and feeling sad, even guilty. I have been in the path of totality eight times. FOUR have been clouded out. The latest one was because a clear sky turned to clouds in twenty lousy minutes before totality. I had to wait thirteen years between my first cloudy totality and my first clear totality. Then in 2021, I led an expedition cruise ship of 250 people into cloud. Man, I felt so guilty. Some people on the ship had spent their life savings.

Missing totality can leave some grieving. There can be anger, blame, and regret. We wish things had been different, and we feel useless. Like it was all for nothing.

You wanted your eclipse story to have the perfect ending in Rochester, as I did in Texas. But you will be in a path of totality again. So will I. It will be in a distant land, and I promise it will be all the more epic because of what happened on Monday.

Eclipses are but brief moon shadows. They only have meaning because of people like us. They only have legacies because of people like you.

—Jamie Carter to Dan Schneiderman,
April 12, 2024[42]

"Seeing this sentiment released a collective breath I think we had all been holding since Monday," says Hillary Olson, the Rochester Museum & Science Center's (RMSC) CEO, after Schneiderman shared the above letter with her. "It was good to hear it from someplace else, a validation for us all, and a digital hug sent when we needed it the most. The clouds didn't matter; the collective experience of it all did."

Failure is an inevitable consequence of any endeavor. It appears as missed deadlines, unraveling plans, or bold predictions that fall short. Some failures stem from overcommitment, others from inaction. In the context of organizing a community,

---

[42] I wrote this note to Dan at 40,000 feet above the Atlantic Ocean on my way home from Texas. Flying is when I'm at my most reflective, and that goes double after a cloudy eclipse. I had devoted myself to promoting this one for years: I wrote over 400 articles on the eclipse, for all kinds of publications. But then I missed witnessing totality myself. After seeing a post on LinkedIn from Dan about his experience in Rochester—and knowing what a Herculean effort he had made—I figured he might need some words of comfort. I hope they helped. I had watery eyes as I wrote them; as I got off the plane and sent Dan the message, I realized that writing it was also part of my own grieving process. —*Jamie*

the stakes are magnified. Communities invest time, resources, and hope. That comes with the risk of not meeting expectations.

Yet failure is not an endpoint. By embracing failure as a natural step toward progress, we uncover the tools to reframe it, recover from it, and ultimately transform it into a stepping stone for future success.

Understanding Failure and Recovery

1. Failing to convince others
2. Preparing to fail
3. Coping with disappointment
4. Coping with the aftermath
5. Reframing failure

1. Failing to convince others

The need to educate and engage people is a crucial aspect of any endeavor, but it's extremely challenging. "It's really hard to get people's attention these days, particularly for something they don't understand," says David Makepeace, an eclipse chaser and filmmaker at EclipseGuy.com. "They haven't experienced what a life-changer witnessing an eclipse is—what you don't know, you don't know."

In an era where hyperbole and overstimulation are rife on social media, generating genuine interest is becoming increasingly difficult. "There's only so much you can do without a massive national campaign," Makepeace explains. "You'd need to be a social media guru to hit every inbox and every set of eyes hard—it's a gigantic effort."

Even for those attempting to inspire curiosity, skepticism remains a significant barrier. "What do you tell a skeptic? It's so hard because totality is so difficult to describe," says Trish Erzfeld. Kristopher Harsh, a member of the Cleveland City Council, echoes this sentiment: "You can never accurately convey how special this moment is to people who are skeptical. Some people just want to shrug and move along."

Many community members in Texas underestimated the significance of the event, explained Dawn Davies, the Night Sky program manager for the Hill Country Alliance in Austin. For some, planning for something that would last a few minutes seemed like an unworthy investment of time and money. Texas had a warm-up event in the shape of an annular eclipse in October 2023. "Members had to overcome the challenges of communicating and collaborating with state agencies and officials, who often denied the significance of the two eclipse events," says Davies.

In Geneva, New York, organizers struggled to convince local restaurants of the financial rewards of opening on eclipse day. "I tried for a year to convince owners that this was coming, but I got two general responses: "No one will come," and "We are closed on Mondays,'" says Debbie Ferrell. Despite her efforts, most restaurants closed, and as a consequence, visitors headed to the supermarket instead. She was proved correct: Restaurants that did stay open for the eclipse had about 300 percent more revenue than the previous week.

A potential solution is simply to begin community engagement and education earlier. "We began our outreach efforts years in advance, but I think we could have started even sooner to build momentum and excitement," says Schneiderman. "An extra six months to a year of lead time may have helped overcome some initial skepticism."

2. Preparing to fail

Failure and bad luck are not the same thing.

Solar eclipses are notoriously weather-dependent. You can travel across continents to experience totality, but when you get there, there's always weather. Although it still gets dark during totality, being "clouded out" means no view of the Sun's corona, a mesmerizing sight that's typically the goal of eclipse chasers. They regularly boast about how they've never been clouded out and congratulate themselves on making shrewd decisions about where to position themselves under clear skies. Defining success in such a narrow way is, of course, foolish when considerable uncertainties are involved. Luck always runs out.

North America would find that out the hard way on April 8, 2024. What locations would have the best weather for the eclipse was a question every leader of an organizing committee across the continent wanted to know the answer to well in advance. Theoretically, the answer to the question, "What is the best place for the eclipse?" was simple: Anywhere within the path of totality with a clear sky for the few minutes of totality. That wasn't much help for planners.

April sees the transition from winter into late spring across North America, and where would be clear and where would be cloudy would only be revealed on the day itself (albeit hinted at in weather forecasts in the few days beforehand). Until then, communities had only climatology, data based on long-term trends. That data, based only on averages, was neither promising nor clear-cut: Texas had about a 50 percent chance of a clear sky, which reduced as the path moved northeast, with Vermont and Maine rated as having a 10 percent chance. These widely publicized figures, together with a generally pessimistic attitude to weather in April, baked in some unhelpful public responses to attempts to spread the word about the eclipse.

Conjecture about the weather on eclipse day was pivotal for communities in deciding whether to plan events or not. "Eclipse chasers made the assumption that Texas would have clear weather, so nobody was going to choose to position themselves right up in the northeast of the path," says Dr. Kate Russo. While planning began for dozens of festivals and events in Texas, there was far less thought given to staging events in Vermont, Maine, and New Hampshire, where the climate was cold and typically cloudy. Similarly, relatively few events planned in Midwest states, such as Indiana and Ohio, were aimed at visitors.

A particular narrative about the weather found momentum, informing predictions. Texas was expected to host a million visitors and receive a $1.4 billion injection as a result, while in New Hampshire, as few as 450 eclipse chasers were expected, according to the visitation estimates from Michael Zeiler, a Santa Fe-based eclipse cartographer at GreatAmericanEclipse. com, who was a member of the AAS Solar Eclipse Task Force. [43, 44] His work was the basis for many community efforts' predictions, though many misinterpreted it.

Zeiler made it clear he was dealing with unknowns. His model calculated the shortest drive paths from over 3,000 US counties to destinations in the path of totality, using ArcGIS software, United States Census data and a detailed digital road network for the United States. It assumed that people who

---

[43] The Perryman Group, "Economics of the 2024 Solar Eclipse," March 25, 2024.

[44] Great American Eclipse, "Predicting Eclipse Visitation with Population Statistics – 2024 Total," https://www.greatamericaneclipse.com/visitation.

lived close to the path of totality were more likely to visit than those more distant. It also assumed that people would travel the shortest drive distance to the path of totality. Zeiler estimated that Texas would be the most popular destination, with around 1 million visitors, followed by Indiana and Ohio, with half a million each.

Many regions used these rough figures to inform predictions that millions of visitors would flood in, only to be wildly off the mark. This regularly happens in communities during total solar eclipses, many of whom are under pressure to justify the expense of planning an event. The poster child in 2024 for overestimation was Arkansas, which confidently predicted up to 1.5 million visitors.[45] "I talked to a reporter in Arkansas about that, and I told him that it wasn't realistic," says Zeiler, who had estimated Arkansas would see between 84,000 and 337,000 eclipse chasers. Another eye-rolling prediction came from Bloomington, Indiana, which announced publicly that they were expecting 300,000 to arrive for the eclipse.[46]

By making assumptions about the weather or using overinflated estimates to justify their efforts in the short term, these communities were setting themselves up for a fall in the long term.

3. Coping with disappointment

About 50 million people witnessed the 2024 eclipse, but where they did so was not as predicted. The main reason why so many

---

[45] Arkansas Department of Transportation, *2024 Solar Eclipse Traffic Management Plan.* Little Rock: Arkansas Department of Transportation, October 11, 2023.

[46] Griffin Gonzales, "Bloomington Prepared to Host Over 300,000 for April's Solar Eclipse," WRTV Indianapolis, March 6, 2024.

assumptions proved inaccurate was the weather. The cloud map on April 8 was completely contrary to expectations; many places where historical data suggested clear skies had cloudy ones, and vice versa. "You could not—if you were Satan himself—design it any better," says Gordon Emslie, a professor in Western Kentucky University's physics and astronomy department.[47] On the day, Texas had clouds and mostly empty highways, with perhaps only 270,000 visitors—a fraction of earlier predictions—while the Midwest and the Northeast states had beautifully clear skies.[48] New Hampshire, where as few as 450 eclipse chasers were expected, saw almost 170,000 extra vehicles descend.[49] "The visitation in Texas was muted because everyone knew a week in advance that the weather forecast was challenging," says Zeiler. "But that resulted in massive visitation that far exceeded predictions in Upstate New York, Vermont, New Hampshire, and Maine."

The reality of a clouded-out eclipse can be hard to endure. Glum looks on the faces of some eclipse chasers are seen in the wake of the Moon's shadow racing over clouds. However, while the luck of the dice affected the perceived success or failure of endeavors and events, for some communities, failure was already inevitable.

Arkansas was left disappointed, reporting little traffic on the roads, despite clear skies on the day, with plenty of eclipse

---

[47] AAS Solar Eclipse Task Force, "First Look at Citizen Science from the 8 April 2024 Total Solar Eclipse," Monday, June 10, 2024.

[48] Cody Copeland, "Eclipse visitors were supposed to overwhelm Texas and its roads. Where was everybody," *Fort Worth Star-Telegram*, April 17, 2024.

[49] New Hampshire Department of Transportation, "Thousands Travel to NH to View Solar Eclipse," press release, NH Department of Transportation, April 10, 2024.

chasers relocating from Texas.[50] Bloomington saw only tens of thousands turn up on the day. Post-eclipse reports had head-lines like, "Where were the crowds?" and " What happened?" as if promises had been broken.

It's a stark demonstration that in planning, there are so many unknowns—and that's something leaders must realize at the outset. If an entire endeavor is built merely on numbers, whether rigorously calculated or not, it's set up to fail.

Not all communities naively staked success on clear weather and the total number of visitors. Rochester predefined success as something other than whether the Sun was visible, which helped mitigate both risk and a sense of failure when eclipse chasers who had originally decided to visit changed course for the clear skies of other parts of Upstate New York and beyond.

Not that Rochester didn't have some issues of its own making that could be seen as a failure. "Out of a bunch of switches to turn all of our outside lights off, there was one that was missed, and that was where everyone was standing," says Schneiderman. "So when the sky got dark, those lights auto-matically came on. There was a massive negative reaction, and that was probably one of the toughest pieces of feedback that I received." It was the biggest thing that went wrong on-site that weekend, aside from the clouds.

For communities planning for any event, long-term suc-cess cannot be based on unpredictable factors that cannot be controlled.

---

50 Daniel McFadin, "While Tourism Bounty from Total Eclipse Didn't Meet Expectations, State Gained Knowledge for Next Time," *Arkansas Democrat-Gazette*, July 7, 2024,

4. Coping with the aftermath

The eclipse passed, and on April 9, 2024, things were quiet again. Even the most successful events can lead to a letdown when they're over, and for some, this results in sadness, disappointment, and separation anxiety.

"I struggled with the aftermath," says Rachel Laber Pulvino. "Even if everything had gone perfectly in Rochester, I think the emotional comedown would still have happened." Many team members compared it to planning a wedding, with so much energy put into something that was suddenly done and gone. "Later that night, I went out with two colleagues to a neighborhood bar, and I remember walking in and thinking, 'Why is no one talking about this incredible experience we just shared?' It felt like everyone had moved on to the next thing," says Laber Pulvino.

Coming to the end of something so all-consuming can be difficult to cope with. "After the eclipse, I completely broke down during a champagne toast," says Schneiderman. "It felt like a bereavement." Many months later, he was still suffering from eclipse burnout. "It's something I'm still working through after dedicating three intense years," he says. "It's given me a deeper appreciation for work-life balance and the importance of self-care, especially when taking on such an all-consuming project."

In Vincennes, Indiana, the eclipse was a complete success, with clear skies and no incidents. Nevertheless, Sarah Wolfe experienced a mix of emotions post-eclipse, including relief but also anger. "I should have carried the eclipse torch a little longer after the event, but I was done," she says. "I was really angry immediately after the event—I think it was grief because nothing that cool will ever happen again. It took about two and a half weeks for those feelings to fade. I rented a dumpster and rage-cleaned our garage." For months, Wolfe struggled to be out in public, where she would have to brace herself for interactions with strangers about the eclipse.

Grief can linger. "Those of us who were so deeply connected to the event had poured so much of ourselves into making it successful, and moving on wasn't easy," says Laber Pulvino. "But I think that's a sign of how passionate we were—we saw the potential for our community and knew what this event could mean, so we gave it everything we had."

Despite the intensity, a sense of not doing even more is inevitable. "Sometimes it also feels like it never happened, and I blame myself for that," says Wolfe. "I really disappeared afterward, and I carry some guilt for not nurturing a post-eclipse public legacy through our social media."

It's easy to underestimate the emotional lows that can follow the highs of orchestrating major events. "I wish we had provided more mental health support for the core organizing team," says Schneiderman. "The post-eclipse letdown was really tough, and I think we underestimated the emotional toll this massive undertaking would take. Having more structured debriefing and counseling resources could have helped."

5. Reframing failure

Many groups see failure as an all-or-nothing phenomenon. They think that if a venture doesn't make $10 million, it's a flop. But that's a foolish way of defining success, and its proponents are likely forever doomed to be classed as failures.

If instead you define an essential component of success in organizing as the very act of bringing diverse communities and talents together to maximize the opportunity, the all-or-nothing sense of success and failure melts away. In the case of the eclipse—and with any attempt to create bridging communities—the success is a lasting impact and resonance that goes well beyond the occasion for which you've been preparing.

That said, the bittersweet aftermath of the culmination of an endeavor needs processing.

"I hope that, over time, people remember the event's success and don't focus solely on the clouds that day. I hope they recall the feeling of the entire weekend," says Laber Pulvino. "Everything we could control was perfect. We had clouds, yes, but totality was still spectacular."

Weather cannot be interpreted as failure—it's merely an external limitation. Those who recognized that limitation in advance were able to plan around it. "One of our main goals was to secure coverage of Rochester and its efforts rather than trying to position the city as 'ground zero' for eclipse viewing," says Laber Pulvino. "I think that was the right gamble because we wouldn't have been as successful if we had focused only on attracting people and media to Rochester on eclipse day."

For many, not seeing the Sun's corona on April 8 was heartbreaking. However, for community organizers laser-focused on bringing diverse communities and talents together and on outreach, that was missing the point. "It's not about me—it's about what everyone else got from this," says Dr. Angela Speck, who, despite getting clouded out in San Antonio, reports that she had a fulfilling experience. "I was disappointed [about the clouds], but most people around me didn't realize what they were missing and still had a great time," she says. "It was a failure from my perspective because I wanted to see a clear totality, but it was not a failure of engaging with the audience."

Failure is always relative and depends on the beliefs of a particular observer—and those in the weeds of an endeavor can lose sight of their original goal.

CHAPTER 11

Measuring Success

"The 2024 total solar eclipse was more than just an astronomical event for Erie, Pennsylvania," says Christine Temple, director of communications at VisitErie. "It was a testament to what can be achieved when a community comes together with a shared vision."[51]

For this city of 93,000 on the southern shore of Lake Erie, the true success of the eclipse lay not in the numbers but in the spirit of collaboration that made it all possible. Countywide, groups hosted various inclusive and educational events, from

---

[51] Christine Temple, "Erie, Pennsylvania's Solar Success: How the Community Came Together for the 2024 Total Solar Eclipse." (Bulletin of the AAS) December 26, 2024.

watch parties at Presque Isle State Park to family-friendly activities like "Zooclipse" at the Erie Zoo. These efforts weren't just about drawing crowds—they were about creating shared, meaningful experiences that celebrated the community.

While many cities along the path of totality focused on tourism and economic impact, Erie's approach stood out. Yes, Erie County welcomed an estimated 100,000 visitors, who spent $3 million, and VisitErie's playful "The Ultimate Sunblock" campaign even won a national award. But the real victory was the deeper understanding of what worked: Erie's success stemmed from the thoughtful engagement of its residents and visitors alike.

"It brought everybody together—they all rallied around to plan this event," says Temple, whose tourism agency worked with the city, Erie police and fire departments, statewide transportation, the Pennsylvania State Police, and the local media. "For a county of our size, it was a community celebration. Unlike larger regions, where big events are par for the course, we stepped up to do something extraordinary."

Among the post-eclipse revelations was an unexpected affirmation: "Nerds make the best tourists." Coined by a professor during a review meeting, the phrase captured how Erie's efforts attracted respectful, low-impact, science-minded travelers. "The Streets Department and PennDOT remarked how clean the area was post-eclipse," says Temple.

These visitors didn't just come to watch the eclipse; they came prepared, enthusiastic, and respectful. It was notably at odds with pre-eclipse predictions across the path of totality that outsiders would ravage rural communities, clog highways and parking lots, and clear stores of essential supplies.

The insight reframes the metrics of success for tourism. It wasn't just about how many people came to Erie. By highlighting the potential of these "geek tourists," the experience gave Erie a road map for the future, showcasing how targeting niche tourism markets—like astro-tourism— could deliver sustainable, long-term benefits.

Erie measured the economic impact of the eclipse, but judged its success based on something other than receipts.

Measuring the success of community initiatives requires a nuanced approach that transcends economic metrics. True success reflects growth, inclusivity, impact, and, most critically, the relationships developed through collective effort. This chapter delves into how communities such as Erie, Pennsylvania, and Rochester, New York, assessed their achievements during the 2024 eclipse. From niche economic and tourism benefits to network mapping, it emphasizes one key point: that valuing and driving expanding networks of relationships is how to create a bridging community and a legacy of collaboration.

Measuring Success in Bridging Communities

1. Defining success
2. Economic metrics
3. Qualitative metrics

1. Defining success

Defining what you mean by *success*, and how you will measure it, is crucial. Communities that choose from the beginning to focus mainly on how much money will be made are ultimately likely to assess the experience negatively. Failing to evaluate the nuanced impact of initiatives, or using only metrics that don't reflect intangible successes such as collaboration and relationship-building, leads to incomplete or skewed assessments of progress.

The story of the 2024 eclipse illuminates that success is rarely captured in a single statistic. Communities along the path of totality reaped differing economic rewards and media attention, but it's the new and enduring relationships between people, often from diverse backgrounds, that will outlast the catalyst.

2. Economic metrics

Predictably, much of the immediate media coverage after the eclipse was about its economic impact, both positive and negative. As was obvious to planners years in advance, clear weather on the day of the eclipse meant lots of visitors and therefore, instant gratification for event planners. For others, "eclipse-nomics" were not so favorable.

The Mastercard Economics Institute reported a 7 percent daily boost in fuel sales across the path of totality, with New Hampshire and Maine experiencing a 26 percent lift in fuel sales, the largest in the United States. Vermont and Missouri achieved 17 percent. That tallies with where clear skies were on the day. In Vermont, the eclipse generated $34.8 million in visitor spending, and the state estimated the total economic impact was $54 million.[52] Impressive? Perhaps—but, in fact, it was less than 10 percent of visitor spending during Vermont's fall foliage season. It seems that orange leaves are more lucrative than a once-in-a-lifetime total solar eclipse.

Also contrary to forecasts, Cleveland, Ohio, had clear skies and unseasonably warm temps—with the eclipse viewed through only slight haze and cirrus clouds. A dozen events were planned around the city, and the eclipse generated $24.6 million for the local economy, with $15.1 million in direct spending and $9.5 million in indirect and induced spending related to the events and visitation.[53] "It was a very profitable four minutes," says Jay Ryan.

Weather forecasts meant Cleveland likely benefited from eclipse chasers relocating from Rochester, but Visit Rochester still estimated an as-predicted $10 million in economic impact.[54] "We recognized that there was an opportunity for Rochester to capitalize on an event that would draw a lot of attention

[52] Vermont Agency of Commerce and Community Development, "Economic Impact Studies Show Boost from April Eclipse, Fall Foliage Season Still Vermont's Strongest Draw," (press release) ACCD Vermont, October 25, 2024.

[53] Emily Lauer, "12 Hosted Events for April's Total Solar Eclipse," Destination Cleveland (news release), September 4, 2024.

[54] Dan Gross, "Visit Rochester: Eclipse Weekend Generated at Least $10 Million in Economic Impact," RochesterFirst.com, June 18, 2024.

and visitors our way," says Rachel Laber Pulvino. "With visitors come spending and the economic impact." The city's hotels were at over 90 percent occupancy, with many museums and restaurants reporting their best weekend ever. "The heartbeat of what we do and why we do it is to generate dollars for our local community," she adds.

Meanwhile, many communities who had prepared just as well as any other for the eclipse received fewer visitors than they had hoped for and were left disappointed. In the Texas Hill Country, where forecasts of cloudy weather resulted in fewer visitors than expected, the economic impact was hard to gauge, given that sales tax collections and hotel occupancy tax revenue are calculated monthly. Kerrville, which hosted a huge NASA event, saw a slight increase in sales tax revenue. "We didn't bank on that because there were too many unknowns," says Julie Behrens, director of finance for the city of Kerrville, to the *San Antonio Express–News*.[55] Kerrville brought in about $297,000 in revenue related to the eclipse, but spent about $440,000 preparing for it. "We really did not look at this event as an income generator at all," she says.

Marketing and PR companies, which went into overdrive in the weeks prior, measured their own financial success in a more theoretical way. Chicago's Adler Planetarium reported $22 billion worldwide media impressions for all online articles and postings featuring the terms "Adler Planetarium," and "eclipse," with an equivalent dollar amount for those impressions of more than $217 million if those had been paid media placements.[56]

---

[55] Ricardo Delgado, "For Hill Country, Eclipse's Economic Impact Was Good, Not Great," *San Antonio Express–News,* August 16, 2024.

[56] Michelle Nichols-Yehling, "Eclipses Across Illinois," (Bulletin of the AAS), December 27, 2024.

The eclipse was better seen as an opportunity to thrust lesser-known locations in the United States onto the national and international stages.

"Being in the path of totality put Cleveland in the national spotlight, with many national news outlets choosing to broadcast or report from our area," says David Gilbert, president and CEO of Destination Cleveland.[57] Several national news stations chose Rochester as their broadcasting site for the big day, but at the last minute, some left the city to hunt for clear skies. However, knowing that was always going to be a possibility, Visit Rochester had a much more targeted media plan for the weeks and months before the eclipse. "We knew we had an opportunity to boldly insert Rochester into the narrative about the eclipse," says Laber Pulvino, a key architect of the media strategy. "Our goal was to position Rochester as one of the best, if not *the best*, places to see the eclipse—a once-in-a-lifetime event for many of us. In that regard, we were successful."

From the beginning, the Rochester team knew effective public relations would be critical to achieving their vision. The city's goals were ambitious: secure national media coverage, generate buzz, and attract visitors from across the country. Articles about Rochester appeared in major publications leading up to the eclipse, including the *New York Times*. "We were also able to secure a fabulous placement on CBS Mornings," says Laber Pulvino. "The host, Gayle King, wore the Rochester Museum and Science Center eclipse glasses. That was priceless."

Priceless, indeed, but difficult to measure precisely, because there's a long-term value to promoting an endeavor or event that goes way beyond the initial catalyst.

[57] Lauer, "12 Hosted Events for April's Total Solar Eclipse."

For many communities, the eclipse served as more than a one-time event; it became a powerful advertisement for what they had to offer. For some, this was an intentional goal.

As Missouri's Trish Erzfeld explains, "I've been sent cards and emails from eclipse visitors back in our area and helped them create itineraries as they return with more family and friends." These follow-up visits are more than just tourism; they deepen connections between visitors and the community, creating advocates for local culture and attractions. "Don't underestimate the power of making a good impression as a city or community," says Erzfeld. "It may bring investments back to your area after the eclipse excitement has passed."

This ripple effect extends beyond individual visits. Visitors inspired by the eclipse often engage in other ways, such as by volunteering, supporting museums, or participating in future events. As Erzfeld notes, these interactions enrich the community by fostering relationships that outlast the event. The eclipse, in this sense, becomes a catalyst for ongoing tourism, community growth, and cultural exchange.

Having seen an uptick in visitation after the city hosted golf's PGA Championship in 2023, Visit Rochester knew that being in the national spotlight in a positive way was a highly effective way of getting more visitors. "These events plant a seed in people's minds about our city, especially for those who might not have considered us before," says Laber Pulvino. In the wake of the eclipse, Rochester was named one of the best places to travel in 2025 by Travel Lemming,[58] an online guide with 10 million readers.

---

[58] Nate Hake, "50 Best Places to Travel in 2025," *Travel Lemming*, November 14, 2024.

By highlighting their unique character and leveraging the visibility generated by the eclipse, communities attracted not just one-time attendees but long-term supporters and ambassadors. This model demonstrates that success isn't confined to immediate economic impact; it lies in building sustainable connections that bring benefits well into the future.

Ironically, many of the same rural communities whose populations were most fearful of an influx of visitors for the eclipse have, since that trouble-free day, expressed a desire to have similar kinds of visitors come into their community. "I was asked if I would consider chairing a move to connect wineries with star parties," says Erzfeld. Astro-tourism is booming as a travel trend, partly because of the eclipse, with wineries and farms that got organized ahead of the eclipse in pole position to take advantage.[59] "We're bringing rural areas together by pairing science with tourism," says Erzfeld.

For other regions, the eclipse was a timely reminder of the importance of tourism to communities and, thus, efforts to promote it. "The total solar eclipse was a once-in-a-lifetime event that gave Vermont an opportunity to show more visitors than ever before just how special Vermont can be," says Heather Pelham, commissioner of the department of tourism and marketing at the Vermont Department of Tourism and Marketing.[60] "In addition to the lasting memories eclipse visitors will have of Vermont, we were particularly encouraged to see the comparison to a busy foliage season because it

---

[59] Portia Jones, "Starlight, Star Bright: The Rise of Astrotourism Is Drawing Travellers to the Dark Skies," Euronews, December 12, 2024.

[60] Vermont Agency of Commerce and Community Development, "Economic Impact Studies Show Boost from April Eclipse; Fall Foliage Season Still Vermont's Leading Draw" (press release), October 25, 2024.

underscores the importance of fall and the economic benefits it brings to Vermont every year."

3. Qualitative metrics

Economic metrics like spending, fuel sales, and media reach are valuable tools for gauging a kind of success. Yet they often fail to capture the full spectrum of impact. While numbers offer clarity and comparability, they risk overshadowing the deeper, qualitative achievements of community initiatives. As seen in Erie's strategy and Vermont's seasonal comparison, success should encompass more than dollars and cents—it should reflect the unique spirit and engagement of the community itself.

Recognizing the enduring value of a strengthened community network, leaders of the Rochester Eclipse Task Force sought innovative ways to measure the impact of their efforts. Rather than relying on traditional metrics, they focused on the invisible connections formed during the process, convinced that these relationships represented one of the most significant legacies of the event.

To visualize these connections, the team collaborated with Andrew Beveridge, a mathematician from Macalester College in Saint Paul, Minnesota. Beveridge, known for his graph theory work on the Network of Thrones website, applied similar techniques to the survey data collected from community members.[61] By mapping relationships within the network, Beveridge could show how connections evolved before and after the initiative.

---

[61] A. Beveridge, J. Shan, "Network of Thrones: A Network Science Approach to A Song of Ice and Fire," *Math Horizons Magazine* 23 no. 4 (2016): 18–22,

The results were striking: a 67 percent increase in the edges—or relationships—within the network.[62] These edges represented collaborations, partnerships, and new lines of communication created through the eclipse project. The graph vividly illustrated how previously unconnected individuals and organizations had become integral parts of a growing web of community interactions.[63]

This approach demonstrated that community impact isn't just about attendance numbers or financial returns. By extension, successful leaders emphasize that the true measure of an endeavor lies in how likely participants are to maintain these connections and introduce others in their networks long after the catalyst. The goal is to build resilient, interconnected communities.

Another important metric for success is access. Adding a virtual option to meetings in the post-pandemic world gave a visceral example of a metric. Rochester's task force had 174 active members who would mostly attend the in-person meetings, but another 600 or so who considered themselves both on the task force and part of the community. The technology used to widen access also created an instant metric to judge the success of the concept.

The Solar Eclipse Activities for Libraries (SEAL) project succeeded because it met its goals; 6 million pairs of eclipse glasses and information booklets were delivered to the public via 15,000+ public libraries in 2023 and 2024. "Since we think that people generally share glasses with at least two other people (often more), we thus estimate that we reached at least

[62] Jamie Carter, "Has Polarization Destroyed America's Communities? No, Says April's Eclipse," *Forbes*, July 20, 2024.
[63] These graphs are displayed in the Afterward of this book.

18 million people with safe eclipse viewing opportunities," says Dr. Andrew Fraknoi. The fact that it was—as far as anyone can tell—the largest outreach effort in the United States was a bonus.

The Astronomical Society of the Pacific began an Eclipse Ambassadors Off the Path Program in September 2022 to prepare 500 communities for the two eclipses, largely by matching college undergraduate students and eclipse enthusiasts of all ages with amateur astronomers.

"Our goal was ambitious: 1,000 participants across fifty states and territories," says Katherine Troche, an amateur astronomer-turned-informal educator from Queens, New York. They came close, with 703 participants in forty-seven states. The goal was to share the excitement of NASA solar science with their communities, in particular, traditionally underserved audiences.

CHAPTER 12

Legacy

At 10 p.m. one night in October 2024—just over five months after the eclipse—two forces of nature came out to play above the chill waters of Lake Ontario. One was the aurora borealis, whose mesmerizing patterns of green and red hovered above the United States–Canada border. The other, evidenced by the crowds of people in Webster Park near Rochester, New York, was the aftereffect of April's eclipse—a renewed interest in science and nature. "There were easily 1,000 people there," says Dan Schneiderman, who, in April, had stood under the Moon's shadow with hundreds of eclipse chasers at the Rochester Museum and Science Center. "Every park on Lake Ontario looking north was packed."

"I saw the October lights from my driveway in the city, but my husband went to the lake, which he probably wouldn't have done before the eclipse," says Rachel Laber Pulvino. "People's interest in the skies was elevated."

The unusual popularity of a sudden display of the Northern Lights was likely, at least in some part, down to the intense work by people in the community who had promoted the eclipse. There was even a direct link: a local meteorologist named Eric Snitil with a huge local following on social media began posting graphics and updated timelines soon after the April eclipse about aurora displays. It's another example of how valuable people's networks are to communities, and in this case, its effect continued long after the eclipse.

"I never thought I would see a crowd that big for the aurora," says Schneiderman, whose efforts to educate the public about the eclipse—and science in general—may have been directly responsible for the high turnout for the Northern Lights. "There's something special about experiencing it with your own community."

> The Eclipse Effect doesn't just mean seizing extra-
> ordinary moments; it also means those moments
> last far into the future.[64]

Successfully seizing on a catalyst to build strong bridging communities can begin a chain reaction of collaboration. Legacy is a repeating pattern of community-building that resonates.

Bridging communities can have a sustained legacy beyond their immediate purpose. The eclipse may have left a lingering interest in astronomy in Rochester, but another legacy is the bonds formed during the many collaborative efforts by new networks of people to prepare for the eclipse.

This chapter explores the various dimensions of legacy, from celebrating achievements to preserving the spirit of community. These principles can inspire new generations and empower communities long after the catalyst has come and gone.

For many communities—particularly those with clear skies—April 8, 2024 brought an instant feel-good moment for communities in the path of totality. "I spent a month afterward asking everyone, 'How was your eclipse?'" says Kristopher Harsh. "Every person smiled when I asked and said they will never forget it, they wished they could see it again, and that they might travel to see another one."

The desire to see another total solar eclipse in the wake of one visiting your home is not unusual, but in 2024, that

---

[64] 2024 was an incredible year for skywatchers in North America, thanks to the Holy Trinity: a total solar eclipse, and two unexpected events — the Northern Lights and Comet Tsuchinshan-ATLAS. In terms of how many people read my articles, it was the most successful year my career by far, with at least 65 million page views. But few would have cared about the aurora or the comet if they hadn't already been gripped by the eclipse. —*Jamie*

sentiment—and the potential legacy of the effort to prepare communities—was scaled up as never before in North America.

It's rare for a densely populated region to be visited by a total solar eclipse. In 1979, one was visible from northwest US states and Canada, passing over 4.4 million people.[65] In 2017, 12.3 million people in fourteen US states were in the path.[66] However, in 2024, 43.8 million people lived in the path through the United States, Canada, and Mexico.[67] As a mass participatory event, the 2024 spectacle was a magnitude higher than most—and so was its potential legacy on the lives of those individuals organizing their communities for it.

How Leaders Should Think About Legacy

1. Why preserve your community
2. Why celebrate accomplishments
3. How to leave a legacy of learning

1. Why preserve your community

For a successful endeavor to go on and do great things, the connections forged in a community must stay strong.

The entire endeavor around the 2024 total solar eclipse was, in part, a legacy of endeavors to prepare disparate communities for the 2017 total solar eclipse. "What's remarkable is how the workshops created lasting bonds," says Dr. Rick Fienberg of the American Astronomical Society (AAS) Solar Eclipse Task Force (SETF). "By 2019, you had people from the 2017 eclipse

---

[65] "Total Solar Eclipse on February 26, 1979," *Time and Date,*.
[66] "Total Solar Eclipse on August 21, 2017," *Time and Date,*.
[67] "Total Solar Eclipse on April 8, 2024," *Time and Date,*.

teaching people about the 2024 eclipse. That continuity was something we aimed for."

It's important to appreciate the rarity and uniqueness of what an endeavor can achieve. "A lot of planning that happens doesn't take a community approach," says Kate Russo, who has examined how myriad communities worldwide plan for an eclipse. "The absolute legacy is that a team working together can create things that go far beyond an eclipse," she says. "It's so important to support and nurture the people doing the things on the ground."

The effect of a successful endeavor on leaders themselves can be extraordinary. In addition to fueling a belief in the power of networking and community, leading a successful endeavor— like experiencing totality—can become addictive.

Debbie Ferrell successfully led Geneva, New York's three-day "Embrace the Dark" celebration. Although relatively new to the area at the outset, Ferrell now has contacts across the city and county, the city council, local businesses, and nonprofits. "I am still in contact with people I worked with on eclipse planning," she says. "This entire program led to business collaborations, the formation of new relationships and the strengthening of bonds within the smaller neighborhoods in our community."

Since the eclipse, she's been invited to meetings with the city, county, and state. "Dealing with the planning and organization of the eclipse event has given me new skills, experience and relationships, as well as numerous conversations about new endeavors, some of which I am sure I will unknowingly sign up for," she jokes. "After the success of this one, I have the confidence to move forward."

The experience of planning for the eclipse opened doors for some leaders that otherwise would have remained shut.

Because of his efforts to prepare his community for the eclipse, Eric Michael "Sully" Sullenberger, a teacher from Russia, Ohio, attended an AAS conference to report on the grant he had received from them and met other educators and scientists. One was Russo. "We're already planning on collaborating about how to reach the harder-to-reach rural audience," says Sully. "I am completely blown away by the power of networking…I have seen the power that relying on others yields."

Some are determined that their personal legacy of collaboration and networking is put to good use. "I want to make sure that the things that I've learned by doing this continue to be pushed back into the community," says Dr. Angela Speck, who spent a decade planning for the eclipses, all the time learning new ways to organize communities.

The endeavor also caused some leaders to have an epiphany about their own local area.

"It gave me tremendous confidence in my community," says Sarah Wolfe. "We can do hard, interesting things. It gave me a deeper understanding of where I live, and that has really been a gift. I treasure that." Wolfe—who has since worked again with some of the teachers she met during her tenure as an eclipse planner—also knows she'll be on every major event planning committee in perpetuity. "It really afforded me new connections with the schools and our public service workers," she says. "Our city's tricentennial is in 2032, and I hope to be around to plan for that event."

Building networks and planning an endeavor can be a cyclical process; successful leaders become engines of innovation within communities, driving further growth and collaboration.

Perryville's experience during the 2017 total solar eclipse was stellar. Over 17,800 visitors came to Perry County, a small rural Missouri community of fewer than 9,000 estimated residents, with $2 million in revenues for the hospitality industry. But it's not just about short-term financial gains. But the lasting impact went beyond numbers.

"I am known now as a great community planner, a wonderful collaborator, and an innovative and fearless leader—there are no collaborations too big or too small," says Trish Erzfeld, who expects forever to be known in Missouri as the "Eclipse Lady." "The eclipse introduced me to people I would have never met, made the world a much smaller place and inspired me." The experience—spanning two eclipses in Perryville—of working with rural communities gave her one particularly valuable insight. "I learned to teach others not to let the size of your community dictate what you can accomplish," she says.

The act of leading communities in endeavors can change people and cities forever. With proceeds from its eclipse events in 2017, Sweetwater, Tennessee, was able to repave a downtown parking lot, take out a lease on an outdoor marketplace, and install a new clock at Sweetwater Depot & Visitor's Center. That's a tangible legacy for the community, but the act of attracting visitors may even have expanded the community.

"We had numerous families move to our community as a result of the eclipse, and one business started out of the eclipse," says Jessica Morgan, tourism director for the City of Sweetwater. However, what Morgan and her colleague Hayley Isbill did next is perhaps an even greater achievement: They shared good practices with other communities preparing for 2024 at conferences and workshops around the United States. "We loved playing a role in helping others know what was coming and letting them borrow our ideas to help their communities—the excitement was contagious," says Morgan.

Not even a year after the 2024 eclipse, Erzfeld's community found itself rallying once again—this time not in celebration, but in response to crisis. On January 5, 2025, a historic ice storm swept through Perry County, snapping tree limbs like twigs, knocking out power for days, and leaving widespread destruction in its wake. And then, barely two months later, a powerful EF2 tornado with winds reaching 135 miles an hour tore through Perryville, damaging or destroying 142 homes.

Perryville's eclipse network snapped into action each time. "We saw our community come together using some of the same tactics we used in planning for the eclipse event," Erzfeld says. "Our emergency medical services people were doing what they were trained to do... but the rest of our community knew exactly where they fit in to help." A network built for celebration had become a lifeline in crisis.

2. Why celebrate accomplishments

If bridging communities are to be sustained, they must be publicly recognized, cherished, and celebrated. Part of that should be to intentionally create happy nostalgia.

The anticipation was electric on the evening of April 7, 2024, as the Rochester Philharmonic Orchestra (RPO) brought the community together for a night that would echo through the ages. The RPO Eclipse Spectacular: A Symphonic Celebration wasn't just a concert; it was a moment when art, community, and the cosmos aligned, creating a legacy as brilliant as the celestial event it honored.

"People lined up out the door, down the block, around the corner, up the street, and onto the bridge," said Bob Lonsberry, a talk show host on Newsradio WHAM 1180, in his show that week.[68] "They came with their children, their hopes, and their good cheer, at the flick of the maestros' batons, for the night of their lives. It was the jewel of the eclipse celebration."

Held at the city's Blue Cross Arena, the event was the largest undertaking in RPO history, selling a record-breaking 7,349 tickets. The program, conceived by RPO Principal Pops Conductor Jeff Tyzik and James Barry, vice president of artistic planning, featured an eclipse-themed medley of classical and sci-fi masterpieces, including *2001: A Space Odyssey*, *E.T.* and *Star Wars*. The centerpiece was Tyzik's original *Eclipse Suite*, a 15-minute composition that captured the wonder of a total solar eclipse.

But this event wasn't really about astronomy. "I will never forget the sight of thousands of people waiting to get in, and the energy that was in the arena," says Laber Pulvino, a key member of the Rochester Eclipse Task Force. "There was excitement, enthusiasm, and joy around town." RPO's extraordinary performance was a celebration of what was accomplished in Rochester, with the eclipse as a backdrop. "I hope people in Rochester remember those three minutes and thirty-eight seconds in years to come," she adds. "I hope they look back fondly and maybe even find an old article from the *New York Times* and think, 'Wow, that was something special.' I'll take a bit of quiet pride in knowing I had a part in making that happen."

Communities that come together to achieve great things want—and need—to remember them together. "Our eclipse experience will forever be one of my, my coworkers, and my family and friends' core memories in life," says Isbill. "No one knew the impact it would have until the event happened," she

---

[68] Rochester Philharmonic Orchestra, "Record-Breaking RPO Concert Was Jewel of the Rochester Eclipse Celebration," April 11, 2024.

says, admitting that she and her colleagues were sent gift baskets by visitors for weeks after. "Couples got engaged here during the event—there were just so many wonderful things that we look back on and remember so fondly," she says. "I always will."

Exactly a year after the eclipse, Sweetwater memorialized its success with an event called "ReClipse" to reminisce. "We buried a time capsule at Sweetwater Depot & Visitor's Center with memorabilia from the eclipse—newspaper articles, t-shirts, postcards and stamps," she says.

Lebanon, in Boone County, Indiana—population 15,000—also put together a time capsule they hope will be opened on February 25, 2343, the date of the town's next total solar eclipse. "The idea of a time capsule just popped into my head when I saw the next date Lebanon will be in the path of totality," says Joe LePage, director of communications and community development in Lebanon. "Since none of us will be around for it, I thought a time capsule would be fun," he says. It won't be buried, but will be displayed inside downtown Lebanon's Carnegie Library. Inside will be promotional items from the 2024 eclipse, from eclipse glasses, shirts and stickers to bracelets and banners.

"Along with those items will be a school yearbook, a newspaper from April 8, and bottles of bourbon, gin and vodka from the Old Boone County Jail Distillery," says LePage. There will also be photos of people, though there is a slight problem. "The photos, including the names of the people in them, will be put together in a photo album because we don't know how images will be viewed in 2343—so I'll add a USB and a disc, just in case."

Meanwhile, Rik Yeames placed his car's "ECLPS24" vanity plate, along with other eclipse memorabilia, in a time capsule at the McAuliffe-Shepard Discovery Center in Concord. It will, he hopes, be dug up on May 1, 2079, the date of the next total solar eclipse in New Hampshire.

Other communities developed visual reminders of what happened on April 8. "We were very intentional in Perryville about having something in our community lasting far beyond the eclipse event," says Erzfeld. In 2017, an eclipse sundial was created for the town's courthouse lawn. It teaches people how to read a sundial and also commemorates the 2017 and 2024 eclipse. The task force also organized for a community mural to be painted in downtown Perryville to commemorate both eclipses. However, what was unique to 2024 was a pair of giant metal eclipse glasses, created with Rainbow Symphony, which will eventually become part of a Perryville Outdoor Sculpture Exhibit in a local park.

Articles, social media posts and TikTok memes may be yesterday's news, but some media has a much longer shelf life. *Totality*, a documentary planned for release in 2026, will put the people who worked on the 2024 eclipse for their communities in the spotlight.

"I successfully pitched Vincennes to the film crew and, much to my shock, they actually came and filmed during the eclipse," says Wolfe. For many individuals and communities, the release of *Totality* will bring recognition and celebration, but also preserve the event's significance and connect people long after the eclipse itself. "The circle of those involved was truly enormous—which was partly the hope for the film," says David Heilbroner, the filmmaker. "But now that the film is in the editing phase, I can see how this hugely diverse cast of characters might well open doors for new stories in what feels like almost limitless directions."

Meanwhile, The Smithsonian National Air and Space Museum has acquired Dr. Tyler Nordgren's work, preserving his posters as a cultural artifact of both the 2017 and 2024 eclipses.

If an endeavor is to succeed and have a legacy, celebrating is essential. Marking achievements, of both a community and of the individuals involved in an endeavor, can solidify the collective memory of a community's success. So can nostalgia. Whether through concerts, art exhibits or time-capsules for communities or by public acknowledgments of everyone involved, creating spaces for celebration helps ensure that the impact of an effort will endure.

3. How to leave a legacy of learning

What the AAS Solar Eclipse Task Force accomplished, and what celestial mechanics offered it the chance to accomplish, cannot be repeated. At least, not for a generation. Although the first coast-to-coast total solar eclipse in the United States in 2017 and the follow-up in 2024 were uniquely close together, something similar is written in the stars for North America.

The next total solar eclipse in the United States is on March 30, 2033, but it will only be visible in Alaska. However, on August 22, 2044, and August 12, 2045, total solar eclipses will be viewed in the contiguous US, the latter a coast-to-coast event. Totality as long as six minutes and four seconds will be seen from California to Florida.

In June 2024, at the AAS Summer Meeting in Madison, Wisconsin, members of the AAS SETF gathered to discuss the lessons learned from their planning for the 2017 and 2024 total solar eclipses.[69] Not surprisingly, one of the key learnings was not to put too much trust in climate data. Festivals in Texas, who had expected large crowds, were left virtually empty. The decision to "go large" had left them, and their communities, vulnerable. "The scope is really important—is going large actually good for the community?" says Russo. It's a risk that perhaps wasn't fully appreciated by planners. "Communities don't volunteer to host an eclipse," she adds. "It just happens—and at some point, they have to decide how to approach it." A different approach was perhaps ultimately more successful in 2024. "Another way to go is to go high-profile," she says. "There are a lot of great examples of communities that put themselves out there." Other communities went under the radar, not promoting themselves in a big way, but got a lot of benefits. It's all about making a sensible decision. "You assemble your team, you develop your strategy, and you boldly go where no one's gone before," says Russo.

Russo underlines that the impact of preparing communities for the eclipse went way beyond the event itself, and nor was it truly about visitation, dollars spent, or the PR value of press coverage. "Those things are really important," she says, but the biggest lesson is the importance of the building of relationships and networks within a community. "If your community development is aligning with how you're planning the eclipse, that's the magic of success," she says. "That's how you do it."

The role of the AAS SETF was lauded, particularly its provision of a structure, workshops, online resources and, most important, the networks of people brought together. Science, Technology, Engineering, and Math (STEM) and other

---

69   American Astronomical Society, "AAS Summer Meeting #224 June 10-11 2024: 10 Years of the SETF," Eclipse Resources, Solar Eclipse Task Force.

outreach activities reinforced those networks. "All of that helped the community leaders feel very supported within their own communities," says Russo.

Some outreach has become permanent. Schneiderman worked tirelessly to educate and excite the Rochester community about the upcoming eclipse, training about fifty RMSC community eclipse ambassadors—all from community-serving organizations across the region—in eclipse education, basic astronomy, and eclipse viewing safety. They were given a telescope with a solar viewing filter, educational materials, solar viewing glasses, and materials for activities. "It's continued beyond the eclipse," says Schneiderman, who in his new posteclipse role as community engagement manager at the RMSC secured funding to expand the program into other areas of astronomy and STEM education. "A big part of my new role is maintaining and growing this network of community partners."

A fire may still remain, but the torch is being passed. As the United States winds down eclipse efforts for a couple of decades, people with foresight in other countries about to be visited by a total solar eclipse are preparing. By coincidence, Australia—where Russo lives—will, from 2028, experience four in a decade. Plans are being hatched. "I would love to have an international solar eclipse task force," says Russo, who will once again share her insights with the next generation of organizers for the 2044 and 2045 eclipses. "It's always about building and reflecting and building some more. Every eclipse is different, and needs tailored planning. But you shouldn't have to reinvent the wheel."

Except that, sometimes, perhaps you do. The next total solar eclipses in the United States will offer new opportunities to apply lessons from the 2017 and 2024 eclipses, but as technology evolves, so too will the challenges and possibilities.

What the landscape for collaboration in two decades will be like is unknown.

"The driver today doesn't know how much transportation has changed in the past fifteen or twenty years," says Laurie Radow, retired transportation specialist from the Federal Highway Administration, about traffic challenges.[70] "But I can't tell you what's happening in the next twenty years...I wouldn't even venture to tell you what the technology will be in three years."

The same is the case with communications. The 2024 eclipse also saw an explosion in livestreams over 5G cell networks, something technically not as easy in 2017, when 3G and 4G networks ruled. AT&T reported that over 1.1 billion MMS messages that included pictures and videos were sent on April 8.[71] Personal livestreams via 5G smartphones aside, NASA's livestream on YouTube on April 8 had almost 12 million views, albeit worldwide.

Does the presence of livestreams affect how many people will travel to see an eclipse—or any live event? If virtual reality (VR) headsets like the Apple Vision Pro are almost as good as the real thing by then—or perceived to be—then visitation for future events of any kind may be dampened further. "Maybe you won't need to go," says Polly White. "With VR, people will say they don't need to travel just for a few minutes of totality." Whether VR takes off or not, the nature of interacting with

[70] AAS Solar Eclipse Task Force, "Lessons Learned from Plans and Preparations for the 2017-2024 Solar Eclipses," Tuesday, June 11, 2024.
[71] Chris Sambar, "Eclipsing Expectations: AT&T's Network Stayed Bright During Solar Eclipse," AT&T (blog), last modified April 10, 2024.

content will likely be different. "The very notion of the internet might be very different by then," says Michael Zeiler. "It'll be an immersive spatial experience."

Whether or not VR reduces the need for physical travel to eclipses is unknown, but the nature of collaboration is bound to shift with advances in communication.

What the world will always need, however, is collaborators. Thanks to these eclipses, there is a new generation of experts. "I've had people send me materials they want to be brought up in 20 years for the next eclipses in 2044 and 2045," says Schneiderman. "It's weird to think about keeping an archive like that. But I know in the back of my mind I am thinking ahead because I'll be one of the few organizers still around or still fairly active in the field."

Do bridging communities have an enduring impact? While it may be challenging to measure when people collaborate and succeed together, they can create a ripple effect that resonates.

For many people collaborating around the eclipse, its legacy was a new and different perspective on community. "An eclipse does not discriminate, and one does not have to be a specific age, gender, ethnicity, race, or even species to witness one, yet we each experience an eclipse differently," says Dawn Davies of the Hill Country Alliance. "It's in this shared phenomena of barrierless accessibility and the seemingly infinite diversity of the experience that we find community."

Many thousands of remarkable individuals and communities dedicated their time and energy to make a brief total eclipse of the Sun a singular moment in the lives of millions. We hope this book captures a small piece of, and forms part of, their extraordinary legacy.

Afterword

For a quarter-century, as publisher of KidsOutAndAbout.com, I've had a front-row seat to what makes communities thrive. And I've watched the people who make things happen. They don't wait for permission. They don't worry about status. They recognize that they're in a position to make a difference by envisioning outcomes and working to make them happen.

But in today's world—one defined by relentless technological change, political upheaval, and social fragmentation—many people feel powerless. The COVID-19 pandemic accelerated what Robert Putnam observed in *Bowling Alone*: It pushed people further apart, deepened isolation, promoted loneliness. This book is a counterpoint to that. *The Eclipse Effect* reminds you that you don't need anyone's permission to unite people around a shared goal. Your tools for finding allies, forging relationships, and inspiring action are more powerful than they've ever been; you just have to know how to use them.

The first step is to look for catalysts to fuel momentum. Once you know how to spot them, you'll see them everywhere.

But just recognizing them isn't enough. Leadership isn't about having a title or authority; it's about weaving together a network of individuals who would otherwise remain disconnected. Every introduction you make—every social capital bridge you build in your community—is a powerful, invisible force shaping the future.

That can be hard to see when you're in the middle of it. Community-building isn't instantly gratifying. It often feels like shouting into the void, like pushing against inertia with nothing to show for it. But the relationships you cultivate are real, regardless of whether they're visible.

In Rochester, we wanted a way to *see* the impact of our work. So, a few weeks after the 2024 eclipse, we surveyed our task force members. We asked who they had known before, who they had met through this effort, and how strong those new relationships had become. Mathematician Andrew Beveridge, an expert in network analysis, helped us transform that data into something we could look at.

Task force connections before

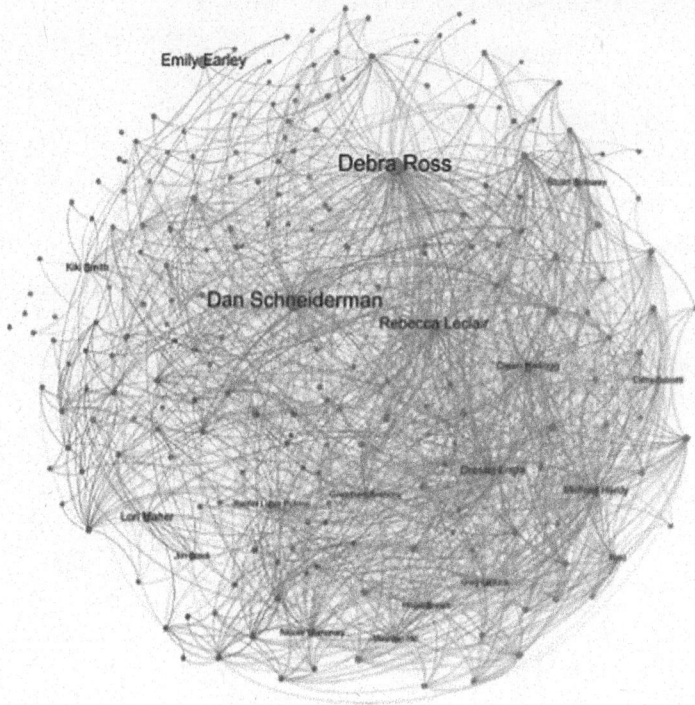

Task force connections after

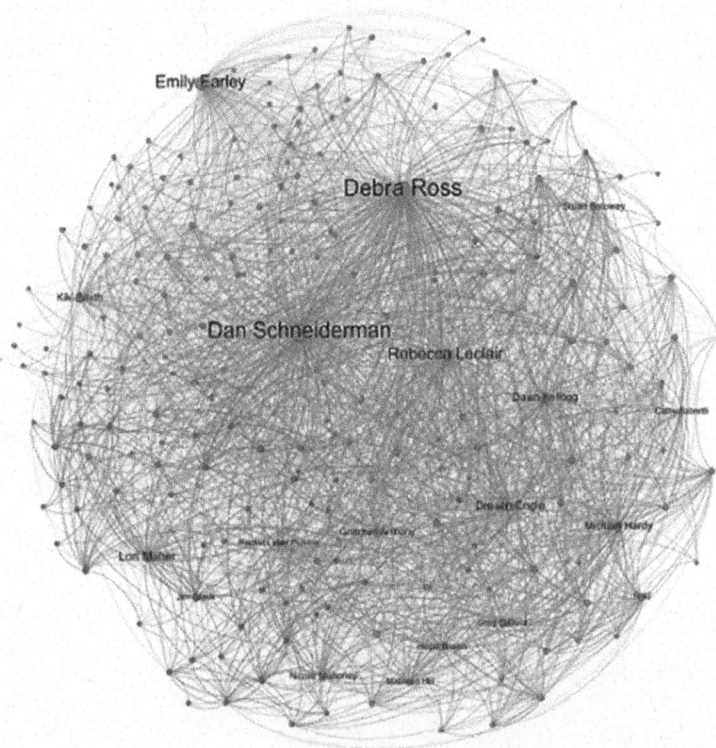

New connections

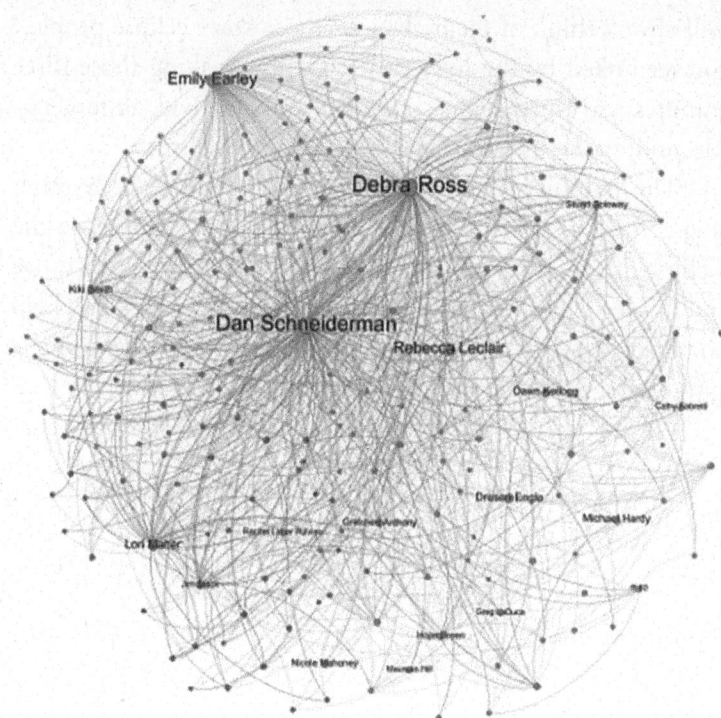

See that final graph? Every line represents a new relationship. Every connection formed in pursuit of a common goal strengthens the community itself. At first, these ties are bridges, links between people who might otherwise never have met. But over time, if they are nurtured—if community members come to see the group's mission as part of their own identities—those bridges become bonds. That's how lasting communities are built. In Rochester, the members of the eclipse task force will always think of themselves as "those crazy eclipse people," forever linked by the roles they played in making those three minutes and thirty-eight seconds of totality vivid, unforgettable, and woven into the fabric of our region's history.

The continental United States won't experience another major total solar eclipse until 2045. But you can harness the Eclipse Effect right now. You won't always have a graph to prove it, but every time you create a connection—every time you help someone recognize the value of collaboration—you are giving a gift. To them. To the world. To the future.

Go find your catalyst, get out your tools, and start building.

—*Debra Ross, February 2025*

Acknowledgments

Jay Anderson, Connie Atkisson, Bob Baer, Michael E. Bakich, David Baron, Roderick Bates, Andrew Beveridge, Allyson Bieryla, Carrie-Ann Biondi, Sævar Helgi Bragason, Kelly Burns, Sanlyn Buxner, Heather Caldwell, Gill Carter, B. Ralph Chou, Michael Clark, Cody Cly, Dawn Davies, Kate Davis, David DeFelice, Angela Des Jardins, Gordon Emslie, Trish Erzfeld, Rick Fienberg, Debbie Ferrell, Kevin Flaherty, Andrew Fraknoi, Ryan French, Pamela Gay, Kristopher Harsh, David Heilbroner, Mark Howell, Hayley Isbill, Janet Ivey-Duensing, Mike Kentrianakis, Rachel Laber Pulvino, Heather Lerner, Lori Maher, David Makepeace, Kevin Marvel, Dan McGlaun, Jessica Morgan, Cherilynn Morrow, Mario Motta, Michelle Nichols, Harrison Nir, Azmain Nisak, Tyler Nordgren, Anita O'Brien, Hillary Olson, Heather Pelham, Mark Percy, Laura Peticolas, Callie Pittman, Laurie Radow, David Ross, Ella Ross, Madison Ross, Kate Russo, Jay Ryan, Dennis Schatz, Freyda Schneider, Dan Schneiderman, Becca Schneiderman, Greg Schultz, MaryKay Severino, Kirstyn "Kiki" Smith, Angela Speck, Dana

St. Aubin, Jim Stack, Jennifer Steele, Eric Michael "Sully" Sullenberger, Eric Szucs, Christine Temple, Mindy Townsend, Jo Trizila, Katherine Troche, Jen Valencic, Amy Walker, Polly White, Vivian White, Henry "Trae" Winter, Sarah Wolfe, Rik Yeames, Michael Zeiler.

About the Authors

Debra Ross is a leader, entrepreneur, and advocate for community engagement, independent learning, and curiosity-driven exploration. A graduate of the University of Pennsylvania, she is the founder and publisher of KidsOutAndAbout.com, a platform serving regions throughout North America that has helped families discover enriching local experiences for over two decades. Through her work, she empowers communities by connecting people with opportunities that foster learning, creativity, and connection.

Beyond her media career, Debra served as national cochair of the American Astronomical Society Solar Eclipse Task Force, helping communities prepare for the 2024 eclipse. A frequent speaker and columnist, she is also the author of *Seasons and*

Reasons: A Parent's Guide to Cultivating Great Kids. She lives in Rochester, New York, with her husband, David, and is the proud parent of two independent young adults.

Jamie Carter is a prolific and award-winning journalist and a leading voice in astrotourism and eclipse chasing. A recipient of the 2023 Popular Media Award from the American Astronomical Society Solar Physics Division for his many articles on the US solar eclipses, he has been a regular contributor to *Forbes.com* since 2018. Widely regarded as the world's foremost solar eclipse journalist, Jamie is the editor of *WhenIsTheNextEclipse.com* and the author of *When Is The Next Eclipse? A traveler's guide to total solar eclipses 2024–2034.* He has also written *A Stargazing Program for Beginners: A Pocket Field Guide*, helping newcomers navigate the night sky with confidence.

When he's not writing, Jamie lectures to solar eclipse tour groups, sharing his expertise and passion for celestial phenomena. His work appears in *New Scientist, Space.com*, The Planetary Society, Live Science, *Sky & Telescope*, *BBC Sky at Night*, and *Travel + Leisure*. He lives in Cardiff, Wales, with his wife, Gill, and cat Edson Arantes do Nascimento.